Louise Creighton
(1850-1936)
Founder of Bishop Creighton House Settlement.

BISHOP CREIGHTON HOUSE
1908-2008

One Hundred Years
of
Work in the Community

by
John Sheppard

BISHOP CREIGHTON HOUSE
IN ASSOCIATION WITH
THE FULHAM & HAMMERSMITH HISTORICAL SOCIETY

Published jointly by
Bishop Creighton House
378 Lillie Road
London SW6 7PH
info@creightonhouse.org
www.creightonhouse.org
and
The Fulham & Hammersmith Historical Society
Flat 12
43 Peterborough Road
London SW6 3BT
www.fhhs.org.uk

ISBN 978-0-901643-05-6

Printed by Hobbs the Printers Limited, Brunel Road, Totton, Hampshire SO40 3WX

ACKNOWLEDGEMENTS

I must first thank all the present staff at BCH, under the leadership of Rory Gillert, who have tolerated my intrusions with endless patience. Jane Kimber and Anne Wheeldon at the Borough Archives and Local History Centre, where the BCH archives are deposited, have as ever been an oasis of calm scholarship and friendly welcome. Of other archives consulted I must specially thank Matti Watton at Lambeth Palace Library and Arike Oke at Toynbee Hall. Rebecca Lackey of the Whitworth Art Gallery, Matthew Bailey at the National Portrait Gallery and Stan James at *The Gazette* have all facilitated our use of pictures in their collections with a minimum of fuss. Also worthy of a shout is my long-suffering neighbour, Tim White, who gets particular gratitude for so skillfully 'removing' the creases and blemishes from the photograph on p 64.

Most of the books listed in the bibliography were consulted from the shelves of the London Library, which remains the best lending library in the world.

This is an 'authorized' history, commissioned by the present BCH Chairman, Mrs Maya Donelan, who has been supportive and non-interfering throughout the writing. No conditions have been laid upon me, and the version of the story in these pages is mine. I am grateful to my friends Dr Andrew Duncan and Christopher Day for reading the manuscript along the way and awarding me a qualified pass mark. Finally, a special thank you to Emily Lane, who applied a professional publishing eye to the piece and sorted my colons, indents and quotes onto a whole new plane of legibility.

For generous financial support in the production of this history, BCH is grateful to acknowledge Goodman and The Mrs L. D. Rope Third Charitable Settlement.

Reading the finished piece, I am horribly aware of so much of BCH history that is *not* there; many personalities who have contributed down the years and many projects that have been important in their day. I can only confess that the choice of what is in and what is not has been mine and mine alone, and if any readers are concerned at what they think are serious omissions, it is at me alone they should aim their distemper.

John Sheppard
Fulham
April 2008

FOREWORD

Bishop Creighton is one of my heroes. I contemplate his fine statue in St Paul's Cathedral and often wonder what his reaction might have been to some contemporary issue. He was the last Bishop of London who could be taken seriously as an original scholar and his *History of the Papacy* is still worth reading.

When he died tragically early it was natural that many people should want to keep his memory alive. His widow, Louise, did two very notable things: she wrote one of the best ecclesiastical biographies which can still be read with profit and she founded Bishop Creighton House Settlement in 1908. This year we celebrate the centenary and I have no doubt of Bishop Creighton's reaction on this occasion.

We are reviewing a proud record of one hundred years of serving the communities of Fulham and Hammersmith. Every institution that thrives should have a sense of destiny and purpose, informed by an understanding of the "story so far".

Where we have come from helps us navigate securely into the future. As the 132nd Bishop of London, (Creighton was the 123rd), I very much welcome this History of the Settlement. It records remarkable achievements and also illustrates the influence of Bishop Creighton House on the wider social scene as Fulham and Hammersmith have been transformed.

For the past of Bishop Creighton House and for all who have worked and lived there over the past one hundred years, we give thanks. For the next one hundred years and for the challenges we shall face, inspired by the example of Mandell Creighton, the word is "yes".

Richard Londin.

The Rt. Rev^d & Rt. Hon. Richard Chartres DD FSA
Bishop of London

CONTENTS

ILLUSTRATIONS

Wentworth Street, Whitechapel,
as seen by Gustave Doré in 1869.
This was the southern border of the notorious
Flower & Dean Street rookery, just north of Toynbee Hall.

FIRST SETTLERS

"To show how man can help man, notwithstanding the complicated
state of civilised society, ought to be the aim of every philanthropic
person; but it is more peculiarly the duty of those who, under the
blessing of Divine Providence, enjoy station, wealth and education."
Prince Albert, Presidential Address to the Annual Meeting of the Society
for Improving the Conditions of the Labouring Classes, 18 May, 1848.

In early August 1867, a young man called Edward Denison - the son of a bishop,
educated at Eton and Christ Church, Oxford - took rooms at 49 Philpot Street in
Whitechapel. He is remembered for this as the first 'settler' - the first person from his
class, from the 'West End', to go and live with and among the people of the 'East End'.
He wrote off to a friend:

> I have no time now to say anything about what I am doing, which is nought,
> nor what I am going to do, which is, or may be, a great deal. I am hardly out
> of port yet, on a voyage which will lead me I know not whither - storms ahead
> probably, but I think I am seaworthy and my compass swings true. [1]

His conviction was that uninformed, casual, indiscriminate charity was doing the East
End more harm than good. He was welcomed to the area by his friend, the historian
John Richard Green, who later recalled his arrival:

> There was something in the tall, manly figure, the bright smile, the frank
> and not to teach," he laughed, as I hinted at 'theories' and their danger. [2]

Green knew the area because, since 1866, he had been the incumbent of St Philip's,
Stepney. The 1860s had been an uncommonly miserable decade in the East End and
both men were sure that the proliferation of disorganised philanthropy was doing little
or nothing to ameliorate the situation. In 1861 there were 640 charitable agencies in
London, by 1869 this number had risen to 1143, and still the problems mounted.
Denison saw clearly the need to engage closely with the people, not simply drive past
tossing pound notes out of the carriage window. In his view,

> The working-man's home in great towns is such that he cannot there give
> himself either to study or recreation. He must have a club, and till every head
> of a family belongs to a club, there is not much hope of the poorer artizans
> improving their condition. Stepney is on the Whitechapel Road, and the
> Whitechapel Road is at the east end of Leadenhall Street, and Leadenhall Street
> is east of Cornhill, so it is a good way from fashionable, and even from business
> London. I imagine that the evil condition of the population is rather owing to
> the total absence of residents of a better class … there is no one to give a push
> to struggling energy, to guide aspiring intelligence, or to break the fall of
> unavoidable misfortune. [3]

One of Denison's first contributions to the neighbourhood was the building and
endowing of a school off the Mile End Road, and he threw himself into the people's
struggles across the board:

My opinion of the great sphere of usefulness to which I should find myself admitted by coming to live here is completely justified. All is yet in embryo - but it will grow. Just now I only teach in a night school, and do what in me lies in looking after the sick, keeping an eye upon nuisances and the like, seeing that the local authorities keep up to their work. I go tomorrow before the Board at the workhouse, to compel the removal to the infirmary of a man who ought to have been there already. I shall drive the sanitary inspector to put the Act against overcrowding in force, with regard to some houses in which there have been as many as eight and ten bodies occupying one room. It is not surprising that the street in which this occurs has for months been full of smallpox, scarlet fever, and typhus. These are the sort of evils which, where there are no resident gentry, grow to a height almost incredible, and on which the remedial influence of the mere presence of a gentleman known to be on the alert is inestimable. [4]

Denison's activities came to the attention of the great John Ruskin, who summoned him and J. R. Green to a meeting, along with another hard-pressed clergyman from the East End, Brooke Lambert, who later recalled the occasion:

Fifteen years or so ago, when Edward Denison was living in East London, Mr John Ruskin asked Denison, John R. Green and myself to discuss with him in his house at Denmark Hill the possibility of doing something for the poor. Denison and Green hit out the idea of a University Settlement, of a colony of men who should do what Denison was doing. The proposal commended itself to us, mainly as enabling men of culture to influence the life of those parts by working on local boards, to do which they were to become rate-payers. [5]

Why then did it take another fifteen years before the first Settlement was founded? Well, Denison suffered from 'lung congestion' all his adult life, caused by 'over-exertion' while rowing at Eton, and died at the age of thirty in 1870; J. R. Green had tuberculosis, broke his health in the East End, was removed to the quiet of Lambeth Palace library and died in 1883; Brooke Lambert suffered a complete health breakdown in 1870; and John Ruskin, of course, was a seer, not a doer, so there the Settlement idea lay, born but not growing.

One of Denison's convictions did bear immediate fruit. As he elaborated in another of his stream of enthusiastic letters:

What I want to say a few words about is the organization of private charity. Certain calculations put the London charities at a total of £7,000,000, enough to give £17 a head to 400,000 souls. The remedy proposed is the union of charities, by means of a registration-office in each parish, all the sub-offices being subject to a central office, which is to be invested with the general control, audit, and inspection of all the charities in connection with it. I think no one endowed with a moderate amount of common sense and of information can doubt that the time for systematizing charity has come or is close at hand. The question is how to do it. We in England are so jealous of our individual initiative, so suspicious of all centralization, so fully convinced that nothing is well done unless done by private enterprise, that we are sure to make our charitable organization voluntary, if it is possible to do so. [6]

Denison was not alone in the urge to 'systematize': in 1868 two papers delivered to the British Association and the Society of Arts laid out schemes; on June 22 the Reverend Henry Solly, a Unitarian, spoke on *How to Deal with the unemployed Poor of London and with its 'Roughs' and Criminal Classes;* and on December 17 Dr Thomas Hawksley delivered *The Charities of London and some Errors in their Administration, with suggestions for an Improved System of Private and Official Charitable Relief.* Arising from these meetings, on April 29 1869, the Society for Organizing Charitable Relief and Repressing Mendicity was founded. Only a year later it changed its name to the more manageable Charity Organisation Society, and the COS rapidly became the central force in sorting out the needs and rights of the poor. One of its first volunteer workers was Charles Stewart Loch, who became Secretary in 1875, continuing in the job up to the outbreak of World War One. He came to embody the COS so completely that one historian has said "Loch and COS were interchangeable terms."

The guiding principles of Loch and the COS were: detailed examination of the circumstances of each individual case, conducted by local workers; an increasingly rigid division of cases into 'deserving' and 'undeserving'; absolute opposition to state intervention as in unemployment relief or old age pensions; a total commitment to voluntary action, on the basis that there were middle class 'givers' and working class 'receivers'. The COS formed their local committees across London in districts co-terminous with those of the Boards of Guardians. The Fulham and Hammersmith COS was formed in 1871, and its first annual report describes how the work was carried out:

> The statement of any applicant for relief who comes to the office with or without a ticket [tickets, referring beggars to the local COS office, were handed out to householders to be given to mendicants in lieu of money] is taken down by the Agent who, after a thorough investigation of the case, makes a written report of it; this having been entered in a book (for future reference) is then submitted to the sub-committees, who hold their meetings every Wednesday evening, when the case is disposed of. The applicant is then informed of the decision. Any applicant in a starving condition is immediately supplied with bread. The general meeting, consisting of all the members, meet on the first Wednesday of every month, at 5pm for the general business of the Committee and for dealing with the more important cases referred to them by the sub-committee. [7]

The Fulham COS later published, for the enlightenment of their subscribers, a list of signs 'used by the fraternity to chalk on gateposts and doors,' so for example, 'a cross within a circle meant *religious but good on the whole.*'

The COS, it has been said, 'came to be universally trusted and universally disliked.' Clement Attlee, in surveying social work, characterised the Society as follows:

> While the system of investigation introduced by the COS has been of great value, it has been accompanied by certain features that have militated against the success of the Society. The fact that the Society is commonly used for the detection of impostors has led to the adoption of a tone of suspicion that runs through the work; a general assumption is made that all applicants are frauds unless they prove themselves otherwise, and this induces an attitude in the COS workers that is profoundly galling to the ordinary applicant, and is apt to bias those who receive their training from the Society ... The attitude of complacency with the bourgeois code of morals and a certain lack of sympathy makes their

charity a hard and unlovely thing, and the Society is regarded by the majority of the poor in much the same light as is the Poor Law. [8]

The Poor Law dated back to Elizabethan times, and had most recently been revised by The Poor Law Amendment Act of 1834, which William Cobbett bluntly called 'The Poor Man Robbery Bill.' It was widely recognised as unsatisfactory, and widely administered unsympathetically, if not corruptly in some places. J. R. Green had no time for the men who ran the system in the East End:

> Week after week charges of peculation, of favouritism, of fraud, ring across the table of the Board [of Guardians] … scenes like these are not calculated to win the confidence of the public in a system which Boards such as this administer. But their social composition, were they ever so well conducted, would deprive them of the sympathy of the poor. No class is so thoroughly hostile to the actual wage-receivers as the lowest of the middle-classes, and it is from this stratum that the bulk of the East-end Guardians are drawn. [9]

Into this landscape we must now introduce Samuel Augustus Barnett. If Edward Denison was the harbinger of the Settlement idea, it was Barnett who brought it to fruition. Determined on work in a hard place, he was assigned by his Bishop with the encouraging words that St Jude's Whitechapel was "the worst parish in the diocese, inhabited mainly by a criminal population." The Bishop knew whereof he spoke: "The first act of welcome Canon Barnett met with from one of his future parishioners on entering Commercial Street to take possession of St Jude's vicarage was to be knocked down and have his watch stolen." [10]

Barnett was heavily influenced by the life and thought of F. D. Maurice (1805-1872), the first clergyman to call himself a 'Christian Socialist'. Maurice founded the first Working Men's College in 1854, and wrote that he was "committed to the conflict we must engage in sooner or later with the unsocial Christians and the unchristian Socialists." [11] This line of thought would lead Barnett pretty quickly to a break with the COS; after a frustrating meeting in 1886 he wrote, "They were just impossible - refusing to do anything except clothe themselves in their own righteousness." [12] The divide, according to Beatrice Webb, was between the 'rigid voluntarism' of the COS and Barnett's 'empirical socialism.' And, she wrote, the split "sent a thrill through the philanthropic world of London." [13] Barnett, with his wife Henrietta, developed his thinking in a book called *Practicable Socialism* published in 1883, which included the then revolutionary idea of universal state-provided old age pensions. That year too, he gave two seminal talks to undergraduates at Oxford and Cambridge propounding the Settlement idea:

> Enquiries into social conditions lead generally to one conclusion: they show that little can be done *for* which is not done *with* the people. It is the poverty of their own life which makes the poor content to inhabit 'uninhabitable' houses, and content also to allow improved dwellings to become almost equally uninhabitable. It is the same poverty of life which makes so many careless of cleanliness, listless about the unhealthy conditions of their workshops, and heedless of anything beyond the enjoyment of a moment's happiness. Such poverty of life can best be removed by contact with those who possess the means of a higher life. Friendship is the channel by which the knowledge - the joys - the faith - the hope which belong to one class may pass to all classes. It is distance

that makes friendship between classes almost impossible, and therefore residence among the poor is suggested as a simple way in which Oxford men may serve their generation. By sharing their fuller lives and riper thoughts with the poor, they will destroy the worst evil of poverty. They will also learn the thought of the majority - the opinion of the English nation - they will do something to weld classes into society. [14]

1883 also saw the publication of perhaps the most famous polemic on the situation of London's poor in the whole nineteenth century, *The Bitter Cry of Outcast London*, which sent a frisson of horror through all sections of society. Published by the London Congregational Union, it detailed with unrelieved passion exactly what life was like for tens of thousands of citizens in the capital city of the world's richest and most powerful nation:

> After all has been done the churches are making the discovery that seething in the very centre of our great cities, concealed by the thinnest crust of civilisation and decency, is a vast mass of moral corruption, of heart-breaking misery and absolute godlessness, and that scarcely anything has been done to take into this awful slough the only influences that can purify or remove it ...
> We must face the facts; and these compel the conviction that THIS TERRIBLE FLOOD OF SIN AND MISERY IS GAINING UPON US ...
> Every room in these rotten and reeking tenements houses a family, often two. In one cellar a sanitary inspector reports finding a father, a mother, three children, and four pigs! In another room a missionary found a man ill with smallpox, his wife just recovering from her eighth confinement, and the children running about half naked and covered with dirt. Here are seven people living in one underground kitchen and a little dead child lying in the same room ...
> But there is a lower depth still. Hundreds cannot even scrape together the two pence required to secure them the privilege of resting in the sweltering common sleeping rooms, and so they huddle together upon the stairs and landings, where it is no uncommon thing to find six or eight in the early morning ...
> These people are entitled to credit for not being twenty times more depraved than they are. [15]

With this alarum resounding in the establishment's ears, Barnett's proposals met with a good reception. Yet in many ways, he was an unlikely standard-bearer; the journalist H. M. Nevinson gives us this picture of him:

> Except for large, deep brown, and very luminous eyes, he had no 'physical advantages.' He was small, frail, bald, far from 'good-looking,' and entirely unathletic, though he played tennis with a subtle adroitness akin to cunning. To people he liked his smile was quick and sympathetic, but he was far from being one of those winning priests who smile and smile, and whose arm seems always threatening to go round your neck ... Nor was he in the least eloquent. In speaking and writing his style was unmistakable but unattractive ... The heart of his power lay, I think, in a spiritual insight delicately sensitive to the difference between life and death. If the brains were out, the thing would die, no matter how splendid and reverend and beloved the poor corpse might be ... We were all revolutionary then, though not so revolutionary, of course, as everyone is now. And yet I remember maintaining that Barnett was the extreme revolutionist of us all. His spirit was like leaven, or like new wine in old skins. He never formed habits or idolised machines. When everyone was extolling and imitating

his idea of 'Settlements,' he quietly said to us, "I do not preach the duty of settling among the poor, I simply repeat the commandment, 'Love God.'" Of all the leaders I have known, he almost alone fulfilled the most difficult duty of leadership: he so hated idols that he was always ready to lead a revolution against himself. [16]

BCH

Samuel Augustus Barnett
(1844-1913)

Barnett's talks at Oxford and Cambridge, for all that he was not 'eloquent', led in 1884 to the foundation of Toynbee Hall. It was named to honour the memory of the brilliant Socialist historian Arnold Toynbee - coiner of the phrase 'the Industrial Revolution' - who had also worked in the East End but, like Denison, Green and many others, died young. Of his last appearance in the East End, it was written:

> It is my privilege to have known Arnold Toynbee and to have been present at his last lecture at St Andrew's Hall, Newman Street, when, stricken by ill-health and shamefully heckled and mocked by a few violent Socialists in the audience, he ended by saying, "Workmen, we have neglected you. Instead of justice we have offered you charity, and instead of sympathy we have offered you hard and unreal advice. But I think we are changing. If you would only believe it and trust us, there are many of us who would spend our lives in your service." After this meeting, this self-devoted martyr to social work in East London and other industrial centres sank into exhaustion. He never recovered from the breakdown and died in 1883 of inflammation of the brain. Arnold Toynbee was the most beautiful character I have ever known. [17]

The ideas embodied in Toynbee Hall proved an immediate inspiration and before the 19th century was out another seven Settlements had been founded in London, not only in the East End, but across the river in places like Bermondsey, Peckham and Southwark, and in the provinces; Dundee, Bristol, Middlesbrough, Edinburgh, Birmingham, Durham, Chesterfield, Liverpool and Manchester. Settlements were set up equally quickly across Europe and Scandinavia. In America, beginning with the Neighbourhood Guild in New York's Lower East Side in 1886, the idea spread to Boston and Chicago, where the famous Hull House, founded in 1889, became the exemplar of a particular American brand of Settlement, unencumbered by a centuries-old class system, and able from its inception to focus its activities on helping immigrants and refugees in a way that only became relevant in the UK decades later with the break-up of Empire.

By 1921, when the first conference of British Settlements took place, there were 61 bodies represented. Some were avowedly religious; Anglican, Methodist, Catholic, Congregationalist, Presbyterian, Quaker or Jewish. Most were non-denominational, like Toynbee Hall, not limiting their message to a specific creed. A few were exclusively Ladies' Settlements, the first founded in Blackfriars in 1887 by a Miss Grüner. These came in practice to have more to do with child welfare issues, and to show in their work a quality of 'compassion' somehow expected of women more than men. Different Settlements pioneered particular strands: Mansfield House offered the first Poor Man's Lawyer scheme, Mary Ward House set up the first play centres in London, and the Blackfriars Settlement founded an Advice Centre that was, in effect, the first Citizens' Advice Bureau.

Settlements arose from a new awareness about poverty and misery in great towns. They were designed to appeal especially to the educated classes, where earlier philanthropy had simply been handed down from the upper and middle classes. Now the equality between social worker and client was to be regarded as a basic principle. William Beveridge, a Toynbee Hall resident in the early 1900s, wrote from there to his mother, "[Settlements] represent simply a protest against the sin of taking things for granted, in particular taking one's own social position or conditions for granted. No man can really be a good citizen who goes through life in a watertight compartment of his own class." [18] Beveridge was as interested in the effect of settlements on their residents as on the locals among whom they lived. For him, his time at Toynbee Hall began the thinking process that would lead to his crowning achievement, the 1942 report on *Social Insurance and Allied Services*, followed by *Full Employment in a Free Society* in 1944, which together became known as the Beveridge Plan, the birth of the modern welfare state. Reviewing a history of Toynbee Hall's first fifty years, he wrote, "A University Settlement is or shall be less a place of permanent residence than a college to pass through; it shall be a school of post-graduate education in humanity." [19]

Barnett's original vision had Toynbee Hall as the nucleus of a 'University of the East End', and if one studies the lecture lists there in the 1880s and 1890s it is clear that it was possible to learn to a very sophisticated level across a wide range of the academic curriculum. This aspect of Toynbee Hall's work only withered away with the arrival of polytechnics and evening schools, but for a time until the mid-90s, it must have felt like an annexe to the lecture theatres at Oxford. London's great chronicler of the day, Walter Besant, characterized the fare on offer as follows:

> These lectures are not, if you please, given by the 'man in the street'; the lecturers are the most distinguished men in their own lines to be found; there is no talking 'down' to the Whitechapel audience; these serious faces show that they are here to be taught, if the lecturer has anything to tell them, or to receive suggestions and advice; they are all of the working-class; they are far more appreciative than the audiences of the West End; they read and think; they have been trained and encouraged to read and think by Canon Barnett for many years; they are very much in earnest, and they do not come with vacuous minds. [20]

This unabashed cultural onslaught had been pioneered by Edward Denison in his time in Philpot Street:

> I delivered my inaugural address last night to a much larger audience than I had expected - between twenty-five and thirty - all working men. I indulged them largely with quotations from Wordsworth, Tennyson, and even Pope, which they delight to hear. I suppose the rhythm and cadence tickles their ear, and somehow helps to lift their fancy to a higher level. [21]

A quarter of a century on, Denison's solo efforts had been replicated many times and 'lifting their fancy to a higher level' was in full swing. Consider for instance, the evening of 18 March 1892, when, the *Toynbee Record* tells us, "A crowded and responsive meeting of the Toynbee Travellers' Club assembled to hear a lecture from the Bishop of Peterborough on 'Rome of the Renaissance.' Dr Creighton gave a most brilliant and interesting address, which rallied the waverers and confirmed the faithful." [22] On other occasions, Dr Creighton talked about 'Florence in Savonarola's Time,' 'The Coming of the Friars,' 'Perugia and Assisi,' and 'The Morality of History'. One of his audience recalled these talks later to Mrs Creighton, "It is impossible to give an idea of the stream of light which flowed from them." [23] Pressure of work when he was promoted from Peterborough to London meant the Bishop had to drop the lectures, but he was still a regular dinner guest, as he wrote to his niece Winifred on 9 April 1897, "Last night I went to dine at Toynbee Hall, and talked to an assembly of Trade Unionists and Socialists about education, and then we had a discussion." [24]

Later that year, The Toynbee Travellers' Club were guests for tea of the new Bishop of London and Mrs Creighton at Fulham Palace. The Creightons, if not *engaged* in the Settlement movement, were clearly sympathetic...

***

THE CREIGHTONS

"In my memory Mandell Creighton appears as the subtlest, broadest-based and, I must add, the most elusive intellect, as well as one of the most loveable characters that I have come across in my journey through life."

Beatrice Webb [1]

When Queen Victoria asked Mandell Creighton why he had turned down the invitation to write her biography, he replied, "Your Majesty should not have made me a bishop." Mandell had made his mark first as a historian, but a sense of duty meant he could not or would not ignore the calling of the Church. Louise, his wife, recalled an occasion during his time as Canon of Worcester when they were strolling by the river and he remarked, "I should like to put a special petition in the Litany that I might be saved from becoming a bishop." [2] He foresaw that this elevation, regarded by all his friends as inevitable, would thwart his work as an historian; a couple of years later, by now promoted to the See of Peterborough, he wrote of himself, "My life has been that of a man who tries to write a book, and is the object of a conspiracy to prevent him from doing so." [3]

Mandell was born 5 July, 1843, in Carlisle, Cumberland, the eldest son of Robert Creighton, a successful cabinet-maker. His mother Sarah was of yeoman stock, and her family name was given to him as a Christian name. From a very early age he was marked out as exceptionally bright; his school nickname was 'Homer', and when, with a certain inevitability, he won a Scholarship to Merton College, Oxford, he was quickly dubbed 'The Prof' - and this in a town stuffed with professors. In 1866 he took a First in Greats and was elected a Fellow of Merton, where he commenced a period of sparkling tutorials and the re-invigoration of the college's intellectual life. A contemporary recalled his impact, "I remember the rapidity with which he rose to be the dominant spirit in his College. Merton was already a brilliant, active, lively, sociable College; but when he came to join the Common Room, he seemed to step easily into the first place." [4]

The intellectual vogue in the Oxford of the 1860s, inspired above all by the publication of Darwin's *Origin of Species* in 1859, was a movement away from traditional Christianity towards at least agnosticism, if not in some cases outright atheism. But Mandell, ever his own man, was going in quite the opposite direction; he steered towards the high church. This period was recalled by Canon Scott Holland preaching at Mandell's Memorial Service in 1901:

He took his stand for God and made his great decision at the extreme hour of intellectual tension, when the panic roused by the new criticism was at its height, and when the victorious efficacy of the scientific and critical methods appeared to have swept the field. It is difficult for us now to gauge the dismay of that bad hour. At the close of the sixties it seemed to us at Oxford almost incredible that a young don of any intellectual reputation for modernity should be on the Christian side. And Creighton by temperament lay open to the full force of the prevailing movement. No one could be more acutely sensitive to all that the critical spirit had to say. No one lent himself more freely to the aesthetic and other non-Christian influences of that distracted time. Yet, in spite of the swirling flood in which he found himself plunged, his inner steadiness of thought and will kept the balance. [5]

He was ordained in 1870, and at the time saw this simply as another component of his intellectual life; he would, he thought, be tutoring and researching at Merton for indefinite years to come.

Every era at Oxford has its star lecturer, the person whose discourses are packed out with curious people drawn from across all the different faculties. Mandell was highly regarded as a lecturer, but in the late 1860s and early 1870s, the palm undoubtedly went to John Ruskin. It was on 9 February, 1871, at one of Ruskin's lectures, on 'Light and Shade,' that Mandell noticed his friend Humphry Ward chatting with an unfamiliar woman and afterwards asked him, "Who is that girl who has the courage to wear yellow?"

Louise von Glehn was twenty, the youngest daughter and tenth of twelve children born to Robert von Glehn, a prosperous German merchant and his Scottish wife, Agnes, now settled at Peak Hill Lodge in Sydenham. Louise had recently been one of a group of six to pass the first London University exam ever open to women. She was young, attractive, serious, cultivated, intelligent and well-to-do. Within three weeks she and Mandell were secretly engaged, though he, in a curiously old-fashioned scruple, would not think it proper to go public until he had secured her father's permission. Just eleven months after first sight of each other, they married on 8 January 1872. There was a period of uncertainty about what marriage would do to Mandell's Fellowship at Merton, which had hitherto required its High Table to be celibate. But they need not have worried; the college was so keen to retain him that the Statutes were altered, over-riding the protests of the older dons, and Mandell could continue, Merton's first married Fellow.

Louise fell happily straight into the Oxford life and within two years their first two children were born. Comfortably provided for, Louise was free to join in the intellectual and social life of the university, which she loved. But Mandell was chafing; already shaping in his mind was the outline of what was to prove his greatest work of historical writing, a *History of the Papacy*, and he knew that to get started on this he needed a change of environment. The living at Embleton, on the remote Northumberland coast, which was in the gift of Merton College, was vacant. On a visit to his father, Mandell wrote to Louise, knowing he needed to be very persuasive to bring her round to this 'exile':

ADVANTAGES OF OXFORD	ADVANTAGES OF EMBLETON
1. Stimulus of intellectual society.	1. Quiet and energy undisturbed by struggles concerning your work.
2. Facilities of consulting libraries.	2. Opportunity of uninterrupted work all the year round, and concentration of intellectual energy on one subject.

We cannot look to Oxford as our abiding resting-place. Shall we let ourselves grow old in its allurements before we quit it? That is the worst of it; literary application and tutoring don't run side by side ... The tendency of Oxford is to make me a teaching drudge, and prevent me from being a literary student. [6]
Altogether he wrote three times in four days rehearsing the arguments, and of course, as she was to do at every future turning point in the marriage, Louise bowed to his wishes. In 1875, Mandell became the Vicar of Embleton.

Embleton gave him the comparative peace he desired, but it should not be thought that he used the living as a sinecure while getting on with his book. He was a hard-working vicar, as his entry in the *Blackwell Dictionary of Historians* says, "Creighton was drawn to pastoral work for two reasons. First he had a deep, abiding concern for people. He was interested in them as individuals. Second, he was a man of affairs. He liked to get things done." [7]

Edmund Gosse, who knew him well, gives us a vivid picture of the vicar about his work:
Embleton has a fishing suburb on the sea, called Craster. This was a fever-ridden village, sunken in dirt and negligence. Creighton, disregarding the growls of the indignant and suspicious fishermen, took it vigorously in hand, drained it, cleaned it, held services there, founded - what had never been dreamed of - a village school. We used to tell him that Craster was his spoilt child. He seemed to hover about it, washing its unwilling face, and combing its wilful tangles. One watched him pounce down to see what Craster was doing, and sweep along the street of it like a winged person, ready to castigate or caress. [8]

The life of a country vicar's wife was an education too for Louise; many years later she would recall, "We did not visit together though we used to walk together to a particular village and then separate to visit different families and meet again to walk home together and talk over what we had discovered ... Visiting taught much about the lives of the people and certainly enlarged my experience and I hope my sympathies." [9]

In between swooping visits to Craster and educative holidays in Italy, Mandell got on with his researches, and the first two volumes of the *History of the Papacy* were published in 1882. Louise recalled the books' reception:
All critics alike agreed in recognising his absolute impartiality, some blamed him in consequence for being colourless. He was criticised both for not praising enough, and for not blaming enough. But he would not own to any desire to whitewash. "I don't think I try to whitewash John XXIII," he wrote, "I only remove some of the black." ... Probably most readers would agree with the

judgment of the writer in the *Quarterly Review*, "Cold and dry as much of the *History of the Papacy* is, it is never dull; for the working of a keen intellect on a problem of great intricacy makes itself apparent on every page." [10]

Briefly to digress forward; when the next two volumes of the *History* were published, in 1887, they were reviewed by no less a grandee than Lord Acton, who took issue strenuously with Mandell's studied neutrality. Mandell had refused to condemn even the most profligate and dissipated of the Renaissance Popes, the Borgia Alexander VI, saying of him; "The exceptional infamy that attaches to him is largely due to the fact that he did not add hypocrisy to his other vices." [11] This was too much for Acton, who worked himself up to produce possibly the most famous maxim in British history:

> I cannot accept your canon that we are to judge Pope and King unlike other men, with a favoured presumption that they did no wrong. If there is any presumption, it is the other way, against holders of power, increasing as the power increases. Historic responsibility has to make up for the want of legal responsibility. *Power tends to corrupt, and absolute power corrupts absolutely.* [12]

After Embleton, Mandell briefly returned to academe, accepting the honour of being the inaugural Dixie Professor of Ecclesiastical History at Cambridge, along with a Fellowship at Emmanuel College. But within a year he was having to combine this with being a Canon at Worcester, the next step up the ladder of the Anglican hierarchy, leading, his friends already foresaw, to a bishopric. Whatever his misgivings, Mandell was ever obedient and he perhaps knew that his days as a devoted student of history were numbered.

For both Mandell and Louise, Worcester was their first encounter with the unpleasant realities of urban society in the second half of the nineteenth century; living in Oxford, Embleton and Cambridge hitherto had been privileged and cut off from the squalor that characterised so much town life. Even the grubby little patch of Craster that Mandell had personally cleaned up was no preparation for the sheer volume of poverty they found in the environs of Worcester's china and glove factories. It was to provoke Mandell's first public statement of concern for the underclasses, in a sermon preached to a Sanitary Congress at Worcester in 1889:

> God made the water to trickle from many fountains, and gather into the streams that flow into the rivers. God sent it forth pure and clear, a refreshment unto man. Modern industry has polluted the sources of our streams, has filled them with noxious products, has rendered them turbid and discoloured, no longer a joy to the eye, no longer fitted to supply man's needs. Modern industry has drawn men to live together in greater masses than ever before, and by bringing men together in masses has brought about conditions which are in many cases hurtful to health, and which in all cases tend to rob life of its simple and natural pleasures … The conditions under which life is lived, the unwholesome air of the factory, the crowded workshop, the ill-ventilated room, all those things that rob the body of its vigour, how they must react also upon the soul! You heard in the Epistle this morning of the works of the flesh - uncleanliness, hatred, variance, drunkenness, revelling. Do not these things, think you, come very largely from, and are they not greatly affected by, the physical conditions under which life is lived? If we allow health and strength to be slowly sapped by want of consideration for the actual physical conditions under which life is lived, surely

we are responsible for bringing ruin to the young soul, for not doing our part to clear the weeds from the fair garden of God, so that every plant that is sown therein by the grace of His Holy Spirit, may grow into all the beauty which the grace of God alone can give us. Yes, there is much to be done. [13]

Many of Mandell's contemporaries noted his love of paradox; his conversation was littered with them, often covering subtle thought with a surface glitter. Perhaps his most famous and provocative remark in this line (earning him his one entry in the *Oxford Dictionary of Quotations*) was "No people do so much harm as those who go about doing good." He was contemptuous of politicians and politics, he was opposed to female suffrage, and he was a pillar of the establishment, yet he saw a definite and inevitable revolutionary future that, coming from him, astonished his listeners:

I do not mean that a cut-and-dry system of Socialism will be accepted by the State in the lifetime of any one of us; but I do think that legislation will more and more assume a socialistic bias and rightly so, and that the rights of the individual will be less regarded when they evidently clash with the welfare of the people as a whole. [14]

More immediately there were problems in Worcester for which a possible solution presented itself, as Louise later recalled:

Experience of the way in which a cathedral town was beset by beggars and impostors of every kind led Creighton to desire to introduce the Charity Organisation Society into Worcester. After some deliberation a public meeting was called to start a branch on January 10, 1890, at which he produced the rules that had been drafted by a provisional committee for the Society. He said that the Society aimed to be "decidedly positive in character, that one of its main objects was the definite and actual improvement of the poor… It wished to be the servant of other institutions, to work without pedantry, beginning in humility, and with the desire to learn in what way it could be most useful." He took personal interest in the working of the Society, and whenever he was in Worcester attended the weekly meetings of the committee. [15]

Louise too, while ever deferring to her husband ('Max' as he was known to family and friends), was finding a role for herself, initially in the thankless task all too often thought of as 'women's work', parish visiting:

I had a district in Barnwell, rather a grim proceeding, a long unlovely street, and I did not feel it easy to make friends with people with whom I had no defined relationship. I hated standing knocking at a door, waiting till someone opened, uncertain of the reception I might get; but I made friends with some of the families and hope that I may have been able to be of some little use to them … Later Mrs I. W. Clark, who had a successful mothers' meeting, decided to start a Mothers' Union, and got a large meeting together which was addressed by myself and Lady Frederick Cavendish. After that I was asked to go to several places in the neighbourhood and speak to gatherings of mothers. It was just then that Mrs Mary Sumner was starting the Mothers' Union, but our first meetings had no connection with her. I also … helped sometimes with a girls' club. Talking to working class mothers made me feel how much something of the same kind was needed by more educated mothers; so with some friends I started a mothers' discussion society. [16]

It is typically honest of her to admit that actual contact with the working classes did not come easily and around this time she began to discover a métier for direction, for delegating, for chairmanship …

"My connection with the NUWW [National Union of Working Women] brought me many new friends, opened my eyes to many different kinds of work that were going on, and in general proved a most instructive and enlightening experience. It added greatly to my opportunities for public speaking of all kinds, and developed my capacity for business and organization. I discovered that I could be a very good chairman. I could keep order, and get things to go briskly, with plenty of life and go, and could keep people contented and amused. It was a pretty exacting task to chair one of the long executive committees, with a vast number of subjects coming up and many eager, clever women all anxious to speak. To preside at the big conferences was in its way even more exacting, but also more exciting. I enjoyed it and enjoyed the credit I won, and the praises and compliments showered upon me. I am afraid I had plenty of vanity and loved praise and being made much of; but my pride helped me to hide my vanity, and I was never gushing, and hated anything like flattery. But it has taken long to grow indifferent to what others think of me, and to lose consideration of myself and of the effect I am producing in the work I am doing. The victory is by no means won yet, and I do not suppose it ever will be, and yet as the years pass I grow more and more convinced that to achieve anything like the character of a follower of Christ one must lose oneself. [17]

On 12 February, 1891, Mandell received a letter at his Cambridge house from Lord Salisbury, the Prime Minister, saying he had the Queen's permission to nominate him to the Diocese of Peterborough. Louise recalled:

I was in London with some of the children on the day Lord Salisbury's letter came. When I returned late in the evening, I was surprised at his restless manner as he paced about the room while we had our supper. As soon as the children had gone to bed he said to me, "Well, the blow has fallen." I asked whether he felt clear that he was bound to accept. He answered that he was afraid so, that when a man had once entered a service, he must not shrink from the call to advance in it, however unwelcome it might be … I do not think anyone realised the sacrifice it was, for he did not speak of it and he did not show it. The brightness, the sense of power, the living energy which he carried into public life, would naturally lead to the belief that in it he found his chief joy. Only those who knew him best understood that it was the student's life which he really craved for. [18]

Mandell's move to Peterborough was particularly tough for Louise; in their life together so far they had never been apart for long, and most days they had found time to walk and talk, share concerns, discuss ideas. Now Mandell was running a large and disparate Diocese, which he conscientiously explored from end to end, being away three or four days a week, as well as having to be in London regularly for convocations, giving lecture series at both Oxford and Cambridge, and, exotically, being chosen the Church of England's representative at the coronation of Tsar Nicholas II in 1896. Louise could not go on this trip because the Russian bishops were not married and her presence would have been quite out of place. She recalled, "I felt the parting very keenly. I knelt down in his study asking him to bless me before he went; and had many foolish fears and anxieties during his absence." [19]

It should not be supposed that Louise was simply home-making for Mandell, and leaving 'public life' to him. Apart from presiding over the National Union of Working Women, she was engaged with the Mothers' Union, did volunteer work with the Girls' Friendly Society, and increasingly threw herself into the 'purity question', one of the great campaigns of late Victorian England, aiming to rescue 'fallen women.' In addition, she was in her own right a prolific author of popular histories, aimed mainly at young people, and had produced eight titles before the move to Peterborough, including lives of the Black Prince, the Duke of Marlborough and Sir Walter Raleigh, as well as general histories of England and France. But for all this independent activity, she still felt herself essentially an adjunct to Mandell's life and work:

> I believe that the wife of a public man has many peculiar difficulties. She is not really free to be herself. She has always to consider her husband's position, and the effect that what she says or does may have upon it; and so in a sense she can never really be herself as far as the outward world is concerned, and may be called upon to let some of her powers lie dormant. But she has abundant compensation, and certainly I never regretted for a moment that I had to consider Max's position in all that I did. I was much too interested in him and his work. Perhaps it was only the strong sense of duty which has been always my blessing and my curse that made me feel strongly called to do public work, and yet I could not help knowing that I had a special gift for it. [20]

When Archbishop Benson of Canterbury died in the autumn of 1896, Mandell was one of the names mooted as a successor. But Queen Victoria, though pleased with Mandell's performance at Peterborough ('very able, very agreeable, with a good presence, and is an excellent preacher.' [21]), felt it was precipitate to prefer him over others. In the end, despite his advanced years, Canterbury went to Frederick Temple, and Mandell was translated to London. With Temple aged 75 and Mandell aged 53, the auguries were plainly that Mandell would be the next Primate. In the event Dr Temple outlived Mandell by a year.

London, it was generally agreed, was the most taxing Bishopric in the whole Church of England; the incumbent not only had a host of ex-officio Trusteeships to handle, including the British Museum, the Natural History Museum and the National Portrait Gallery, he also was expected to attend the Ecclesiastical Commission every Thursday, he had charge of all British clergy on the continent, and, above all, London had the greatest concentration of cranks, pests and turbulent priests. Asked once how he was, Mandell replied, "As well as can be expected when every ass in the diocese thinks he has a right to come and bray in my study." [22] Mandell coped with them all; even the man who attempted to interrupt his episcopal confirmation at St Mary le Bow got a friendly handshake; "Firmly fixed in the English tradition of common sense, compromise and comprehension, he held on his way amid the shrieking of extremists with imperturbable moderation." [23]

15

Mandell Creighton
(1843-1901)

Mandell was famous for writing his own letters (he never had a secretary) and doing so while attending meetings of great moment, where he would look up and intervene, not having missed a twist in the debate while the letters got written. They were not always necessarily confined to diocesan matters:

> The theory that Bacon wrote Shakespeare's plays depends on the following prejudice: Shakespeare's plays are the greatest works in the English language. Therefore they must have been written by a very distinguished man: but Shakespeare was a common man without great learning, therefore they were not written by him. Bacon was the most distinguished man of that time; therefore they were written by Bacon ... But we have some positive evidence, which is in anyone's power to appreciate. Read Bacon's essay on 'Love' and then read 'Romeo and Juliet.' It is a question of common sense if a man who could be so frigid when he wrote under his own name, could be so impassioned when he wrote under another name. [24]

Not for nothing did the Prime Minister, Lord Salisbury, reckon that Mandell was the hardest-working man in the country. Edmund Gosse worried about him, as did many friends, "There should have been someone sent to tell him, as the Bishop of Ostia told St Francis of Assisi, that his duty to God was to show some compassion to his own body." [25]

In the first month at Fulham Palace, Mandell and Louise celebrated their silver wedding, and Louise wrote to a friend:

> It is a wonderful thing for us to look back upon these twenty-five years is it not and feel how they have been blessed, and how we begin the next stage of our life with the home circle unbroken, and still full of possibilities for a full and useful life; may we use them to the full, and face whatever sadness and pain the future may have in store with hope and courage. [26]

Louise, being the wife of the Bishop of London, was thrust onto the biggest stage of her life. She added to her already impressive list of Presidencies, and developed a campaign about the conditions of women's employment, supporting Walter Besant's proposal for women's labour bureaux, and writing, in collaboration with Beatrice Webb and Helen Bosanquet, an article for the influential magazine *The Nineteenth Century* in February 1897 on 'Law and the Laundry'. This outlined the appalling degradation of female laundry workers, and called for regulation of the hours and conditions in the industry. At first sight, working with Beatrice Webb might seem far-fetched, but they had been friends since Mandell's time in Worcester, and she held Louise in high regard:

> In spite of the fact that she is a fervent Christian and I am avowed agnostic, we have a warm respect for each other. She is an absolutely straight woman, who never swerves from what she believes to be right - is sometimes ugly in her brusque directness. She hides with difficulty her dislike or disapproval, and so has many enemies, or rather, persons who disparage her and call her 'bourgeois' and thick-minded ... A calm, fine face, a cool manner, a somewhat dictatorial manner towards those whose intellect or character she does not respect, Louise is not likely to become a popular woman - but she will raise 'society' to a higher level of intellectual sincerity and warmheartedness, and make the world value sterling qualities rather than fashion and mere sparkle. [27]

Louise especially took up the cudgels on the position of women in the Church; the reforming Canterbury Convocation of May 1897 decided, progressively, on the creation of Parochial Church Councils, but bizarrely voted to exclude women from election to them. This despite the fact that in most parishes women did a large proportion of the voluntary work, and were already allowed to be churchwardens. Louise was one of the organisers of a huge protest petition at this exclusion, signed by eleven hundred churchwomen, to the next year's Convocation. It was unsuccessful. Chairing a session on 'The Training and Payment of Women Church Workers' at the 1899 Church Congress, Louise regretted that although Church leaders, "welcomed the establishment of Sisterhoods and encouraged means by which women might help the work of the clergy in their parish, they looked jealously on anything like independence of work or opinion for women." [28]

Despite the fact that Mandell now occupied one of the highest positions in the church, he remained his old Common Room self. Even agnostic friends like Beatrice Webb thought he perhaps ought to be a bit more grave, "The freedom of view, the brilliant dialectic, the subtle paradox, which often covered a daring hypothesis - all these were in place in a Cambridge don; they became impossible, or at any rate most baffling, in a bishop." [29] It is possible that his propensity for levity might have prevented his further promotion, but he was never going to change in order to satisfy any stereotype of what a bishop should be like; he genuinely lacked ambition and saw his ascent of the church hierarchy as a simple function of obedience to orders:

> The emancipation of a Victorian bishop could never be as that of other men. The string that tied him to the peg of tradition might be quite a long one; but it was always there. Creighton enjoyed his little runs with the gusto and vitality that were invariably his. The sharp aquiline face, with the grizzled beard, the bald forehead, and the gold spectacles, gleamed and glistened, the long, slim form, so dapper in its episcopal gaiters, preened itself delightedly, as an epigram - a devastating epigram - shot off and exploded, and the Fulham teacups tinkled as they had never tinkled before. [30]

In the end Mandell had a mere four years at Fulham Palace. Laid low on holiday in Italy towards the end of 1900, he came home to face two operations on what is now thought to have been a bleeding duodenal ulcer, brought on by the overwork he so vigorously engaged in, and surely not helped by his heavy smoking. He died on 14 January, 1901.

Among the many obituaries, none was more moving than that of his friend Edmund Gosse, who concluded:

> The most remarkable feature of his face, without doubt, was his curious mouth, sensitive and mobile, yet constantly closing with a snap in the act of will. Nothing was more notable and pleasing than the way in which his severe, keen face, braced by the aquiline nose to a disciplinarian austerity, lightened up and softened with this incessantly recurrent smile. Such, in outward guise, was one of the strangest, and the most original, and the most poignantly regrettable men whom England possessed and lost in the last years of the nineteenth century. [31]

Louise was a widow at 50. The sun round which she had orbited for thirty years had gone. A few years later, in one of her monthly letters to her sister Ida in Russia, she recalled the impact:

> I remember one of the first times when Max was very suffering and ill one night in Italy just before we started for home. Peace only came to me all alone there with no one to whom I could tell my terrible anxiety, for often the worst of it almost seemed that I could not share it with him, as I had shared everything else, peace only came when I had made the complete surrender, realised all that I had had, and that I might lose it, and gained strength if only for a moment and given up everything, and feel that it was God's will. Then afterwards when the worst had befallen me, there came a strange sense of liberty. I had lost everything, there was nothing more to fear and be anxious about, all that remained was to try and be of some use to others in the life that I still had to live. [32]

Louise's 'strange sense of liberty' led her in the first four years of her bereavement to a scholarly ordering of all Mandell's sermons, lectures, essays and reviews for publication[33], and to the authorship of her biography of him, the two-volume *Life & Letters*, widely regarded as a masterwork, which was greeted by Randall Davidson, then Bishop of Winchester, "I know of no instance in which the publication of a public man's biography has so greatly raised him in the estimation of good and thoughtful people." [34] With this self-imposed duty done, she could now turn to being 'of some use to others.' In 1906 she at last came out for women's suffrage, a cause she had previously rejected in a famous petition in *The Nineteenth Century*, in January 1889, signed by 104 prominent women, instigated by one of Louise's oldest friends, the novelist Mrs Humphry Ward. Recalling that Mandell had been against the vote for women, it is a measure of Louise's emancipation in widowhood that she felt able to change her mind. Impressed undoubtedly by the expansion of women's roles in both the Conservative and Liberal Parties, she allowed as well, "The wild performances of the Suffragettes also influenced me. I thought that they needed to be steadied by responsibility." [35]

From the grace and favour apartment granted to her in Hampton Court Palace, she came to exercise an influence in Church affairs that has earned her the accolade from the chief commentator on the position of women in the Church at this period, "Louise Creighton was the leading woman in the Church of England during the first two decades of the twentieth century." [36] Writing her regular letter to her sister Ida in late 1907, she was much taken up with a big task ahead:

> It is all about this coming Pan-Anglican Congress. It means endless committees in London and endless going about all over England to speak … I spend half my time in the train. At first it struck me as a great bore, but I am beginning to see that it is really an opportunity to do what I most want to do, get the work of women for the Church to be more recognised and better done. [37]

Preparations for the Congress, at which Louise was to chair vast assemblies of delegates in the Albert Hall, occupied much of her correspondence to Ida through this period, and it was almost in passing that she mentioned another project, "… in the midst of it all I am trying to get our Fulham Settlement into order. It is being painted and papered now and we have to collect the money for it, and now there is all the furniture to be got. I hope it will be ready to be opened next month." [38]

And in her next letter, "It is all going on very well. I expect it will be a great interest to me in the future and a centre for all the work I try to do in London, but at present I have been so frightfully busy over the Pan-Anglican Congress that I have hardly had time to give to the Settlement. We have made the House very bright and pretty, and the lady who is to be the Head, Miss Wickham, who is a granddaughter of Mr Gladstone's, promises very well." [39]

***

"A PLAN THAT I HAVE
IN MY HEAD..."

"What is needed is sympathy. We should all of us try to feel
something of the Divine love towards man, in spite of his
weaknesses. 'Men my brothers' should be a thought constantly
before us. I freely admit that what is called 'society' is a sore
trial to one's charity ... You never know what you may do if to
your observation you add a readiness of sympathy. Therefore
I say, do not only look at people from the outside, but try to
understand them from the inside."

Mandell Creighton[1]

It has been written, and some people semi-automatically assume, that the idea of a
Settlement in Fulham originated in discussions between Mandell and Louise, and that
therefore it was really his idea. Research does not support this. Louise was the most
conscientious biographer her husband could have wanted, and her admiration for his
thinking was unreserved, but nowhere in his biography, or in any of the collections she
put together of his papers, essays, addresses and so forth, does the Settlement idea come
up. So we must give Louise the sole credit; it was her idea and hers alone. And, since
she was founder-Chairman and a great lady, from now on she is Mrs Creighton.

The first meeting to discuss the proposal was held early in 1907 at St James's vicarage,
Moore Park. In the absence of the first, probably two, minute books of Bishop
Creighton House Settlement (Council meetings up to February 1916) we do not know
all who were there, but, apart from Mrs Creighton, fairly certainly present were her
eldest daughter Beatrice, her friend the Hon Mrs Sarah Bailey (who would be Vice-
Chairman), Mary Lyttleton (who would be the first secretary of BCH) and the Rev P. S.
G. Propert, vicar of St Augustine's, Lillie Road, and Chairman of the Fulham Board of
Guardians. By the time of the first official BCH Council Meeting at Mrs Bailey's house
in the autumn of 1907, Mrs Creighton had, with the blessing of the Bishop of London
and the Executive of the Women's Diocesan Association, taken a lease on Nos 374-378
Lillie Road, and engaged the first Warden. This most important appointment was
broached in a letter Mrs Creighton typically couched in terms that more or less
demanded the answer 'yes'...

Dear Miss Wickham

I was very sorry not to see you when I was at Lincoln the other day, as I wanted to talk over with you a plan that I have in my head. I have long been anxious to start a women's settlement in Fulham. It is as probably you know a very large poor district, more like South London than the East End, but I should imagine healthier than South London and without some of the miserable industries of S. London. The parishes are very large and the clergy cannot get enough helpers for any of their work. I want the proposed settlement to be on rather different lines from any existing settlement. The training of workers is to be a great feature. My idea is to have only a small number of residents, and to have a great many associates, who will come from their homes in Kensington or Chelsea and work there for the day. I do not want there to be much work connected with the settlement itself, but I want the workers to go and work in the parishes around, the whole settlement to be in close connexion with the clergy in the neighbourhood. Some of the workers could do C.O.S. work or be school managers, others could be health visitors, others again district visitors, or managers of mothers' meetings, girls' clubs etc. The more experienced resident workers would direct and criticise the work of the younger ones, and there would be lectures and conferences at the settlement about methods of work etc. The existing Church Settlements have not to my mind paid sufficient attention either to training, or to investigation of the life of the people. I should wish to make all kinds of research and investigation be part of the settlement work.

It seems to me that there is here a great opportunity, both because of the needs of Fulham which are overwhelming, and because of the constant need that church workers should be made more intelligent, and be better trained for their work. My daughter and I are hoping to give as much time and thought as possible to the settlement if it does come into existence, but my daughter's other work makes it impossible for her to think of being a resident there. I know you have done a great deal of work of various kinds, and it has struck me that it might be possible for you to come and undertake the headship of this settlement. I do not want you to answer in a hurry. I am going away on Monday for a fortnight, out of reach of letters, but if after I come home, you felt inclined to entertain the idea favourably or at least not to dismiss it at once, I should ask you to come and spend a couple of days with us that we might talk it over, and you might thoroughly understand my plans and ideas. I think it is a great opportunity for work, it seems to me almost a call for anyone who has the requisite qualities and is free to undertake work. We are going to throw our hearts into it and do all we can to help it and make it a success, and from all I have heard I think you might be the person to help us if you are willing to come.

Yours sincerely

Louise Creighton. [2]

Catherine Mary Lavinia Wickham
(1874-1973)

Catherine Wickham is the pre-eminent figure in the history of BCH. Warden from 1908 to 1935 and continuing thereafter as an active Council member, she attended her last Council meeting on 1 November, 1972 at the age of 98, and died the next year, only weeks short of her 100th birthday. She is remembered in those last years by one of today's senior trustees, Audrey Surtees: "She would be sitting at the meeting, and you might think she had fallen asleep, but then she would suddenly intervene in the discussion and say, 'No you can't do that' or some such, and you realised she was absolutely on the ball right to the end." [3] The BCH Annual Report for 1973-74 included in its tribute to her the following, "Katy Wickham was a most remarkable woman exemplifying in a singular way the qualities of warmth and sympathetic leadership which were, perhaps, more noticeable in the late Victorian and Edwardian eras than they are today." [4]

Miss Wickham was the eldest granddaughter of William Gladstone, four times Prime Minister during Queen Victoria's reign. Her father was Edward Wickham, Dean of Lincoln, who had been born at Eagle House, Brook Green, so when Miss Wickham came to Lillie Road it was arguably a return to the ancestral patch. As a young woman, she had done voluntary work in a boys' club in Lincoln, and this is thought to have determined her on a life's work among less fortunate people. She expanded her experience with periods of training at the Women's University Settlement (now the Blackfriars Settlement) and at St Margaret's House in Bethnal Green. Mrs Creighton had chosen well; not only was Miss Wickham's approach to the work deeply rooted in her Christianity, but she was usefully well-connected to the Gladstones, Talbots and Lyttletons, all families whose support would be a steady buttress for BCH over many years to come.

Having picked Miss Wickham, and having secured a lease on the premises, it was now the priority to raise money, the perennial question throughout the hundred years now being celebrated. The first appeal was made at the Annual Meeting of the Women's Diocesan Association on 23 November 1907, and the members of the WDA, along with their junior associates in the Girls' Diocesan Association, collected £17. The WDA Committee contributed £50, and the Committee of the Lillie Road Girls' Club, already in residence and due to become BCH's first tenants, chipped in £150 in recognition of the substantial renovations required. But it was clear that a wider and more resonant appeal would be required to get the BCH exchequer off to a firm start. Subscribers were to be offered two ways of helping; they could make a simple one-off donation, or, more valuably, they could become 'Associates' of BCH by committing themselves to annual subscriptions and by committing themselves to voluntary work at the Settlement, also, in some cases, by sending goods (farm produce etc) to be sold in aid of BCH. As an additional attraction, Associates would also be invited to regular 'At Homes' with Mrs Creighton and Miss Wickham at which topics of general or current interest would be discussed by an invited speaker, followed by tea, questions and answers. The first Appeal, in which the unmistakeable hand of Mrs Creighton may be detected, was sent out in December 1907:

AN APPEAL
£500 REQUIRED IMMEDIATELY

We are most of us familiar with the "Bitter Cry" of East London, and the attempts that have been made to satisfy it. The public conscience may be said to have been further awakened to the needs of North and South London as well, not indeed as fully as could be wished, but at any rate in some degree, as is shown by the various Settlements that exist in these distant parts of the Metropolis. But West London seems to have been so far almost entirely forgotten. Owing to its nearness to the rich quarters of London, it is vaguely supposed that it has everything it wants. As a matter of fact, however, the poor, overcrowded parishes of Fulham and Hammersmith are terribly in need of help and encouragement, and the appeal of the clergy for more district visitors, health visitors, Sunday-school teachers, school managers, etc., is heard everywhere, and has met, so far, with a very inadequate response.

It is to meet, at any rate to some extent, this great need, that the Women's and the Girls' Diocesan Associations, with the help of others interested in the work of the Church in London, now propose to found a Ladies' Settlement in Fulham. It is to be called Bishop Creighton House - a name which will of itself go far to commend the work to all members of the great Diocese to which he devoted the last years of his life.

The Settlement is to be a centre of Church life and work; its aim will be to send out duly trained and qualified women to help in the parishes around, rather than to start new work on its own account. While there will be a nucleus of resident workers, so as to secure continuity and efficiency, it is specially intended to welcome those ladies who can only give a portion of their time. It will also make a special point of the training of workers, to be carried out by means of lectures and special courses of study and investigation, and by practical work of all kinds, including work in the local C.O.S. offices.

The details of the scheme are still unsettled, but three houses, which it is proposed to throw into one, have been taken on lease in a good open situation, close to omnibuses and to the Hammersmith Tube Station, and we are further able to say that Miss WICKHAM, daughter of the Dean of Lincoln, has most kindly consented to undertake the post of Head.

To fit and furnish these houses for use as a Settlement, a sum of at least £500 is required. Annual subscriptions will also be needed to assist in the support of the Settlement. We shall be glad to have promises of subscriptions to become due in 1908, and we ask for £500 *at once*, to meet the immediate expenses of drainage, repairs, and furnishing. The prospect of the Settlement is most warmly welcomed by the local clergy, and has the cordial support of the Bishops of London and Kensington, and we ask for the sympathy and help of all those who care for the work of the Church in West London, in the confidence that they will gladly respond to the call.

Subscriptions and donations will be gratefully received by :-
JOHN BAILEY ESQ (Hon Treasurer) 20 Egerton Gardens, SW.
MISS CREIGHTON, Hampton Court Palace.
MISS CURTIS, Carnforth Lodge, Hammersmith.
MISS C. S. GREGORY, Deanery, St Paul's, EC.   *December, 1907.*

5

The response was immediate and gratifying; between them two Earls, a Marchioness, a Countess, along with two Bishops, assorted Deans and Archdeacons, Lords, Honourables and Ladies, and many ordinary untitled citizens gave £840-2-9, well surpassing Mrs Creighton's target. She wrote a covering note, slightly coyly, with the Appeal to Randall Davidson, now the Archbishop of Canterbury; "My Dear Friend, Is it wrong to ask you to help us? If so will you throw the enclosed straight into the waste paper basket." [5] He sent £20 by return.

Apart from money, BCH received many gifts towards its launch:
> Messrs Waring most kindly gave the complete furniture for one room,
> the Hon Mrs Sarah Bailey and her friends furnished another, and Miss Gurney
> and her friends furnished a third. Another friend, who wishes to be anonymous,
> furnished the kitchen. Mrs Trumper most kindly supplied a frontal, an altar
> cross, and a retable, Miss Synge gave a carpet for the chapel, and Miss Creighton
> the altar. [7]

Miss Wickham moved in, the first resident, shortly before Easter 1908, and with a flurry of paintbrushes and wallpaper paste, all was ready for the formal opening:
> On May 16th the House was opened and blessed by the Bishop of London.
> There was a large gathering of the local clergy and of the subscribers for the
> ceremony, and they were obliged to overflow into all the rooms of the house,
> as all could not get into the club room. Mrs Creighton first thanked those whose
> generous help and sympathy had made it possible to start the Settlement, and
> then the Bishop addressed the gathering. He expressed his gratification at the
> starting of a Settlement in Fulham, and his satisfaction at having a memorial there
> to Dr Creighton, and spoke of the work the Settlement might do for the
> neighbourhood. He then went down to the chapel and blessed it, and spoke a
> few words to those who had gathered there, and afterwards passed through the
> different rooms blessing them. [7]

BCH's coming was welcomed by all the twenty-four parishes in the Rural Deanery of Fulham - an area roughly co-terminous with today's Borough of Hammersmith & Fulham - except one; St Clement's, the very parish in which BCH was set up, had a vicar, the Rev[d] Richard Free, who was much opposed, and produced a long, rambling article under the heading 'Settlements or Unsettlements?' in *The Nineteenth Century* arguing his case. As far as he was concerned, the arrival of BCH was a personal insult:
> It is little short of impertinence for such a society as a Settlement to establish
> itself in the middle of a parish, even with the consent of the incumbent,
> a society the very purpose of whose being is confessedly to supplement the
> deficiencies of the parish. It is downright impertinence for such a society to
> establish itself in the parish in defiance of the incumbent. In the latter case there
> can be no permanent peace for the parish ... The Settlement of today sniffs at
> the work of the parish priest ... intrudes itself into parishes where it is not
> wanted ... begs the Episcopal blessing on its schismatical doings ... On the very
> day on which I wrote my first letter of protest against the proposed Settlement in
> the parish of St Clement's, I received a communication from a lady who, for
> several years, has sent me an annual donation for my work. She excused herself
> from doing so this year because, she said, she had decided to give what she could
> afford to the Fulham Settlement, as she was sure that this would be the best way,
> although an indirect one, of helping me. There is such a thing as unconsciously
> adding insult to injury ... It is particularly unfair on the up-to-date clergyman, full

26

of many duties and many cares, to thrust on him the petty vexations incidental to incompetence in the Settlement worker. It is gross injustice that he should be virtually the object of criticism and censure by a secret conclave of women who are able to injure him in quarters where he is anxious to be understood and appreciated, and may practically ruin his career by preferring charges against him which he will never have an opportunity of answering. [8]

Mrs Creighton may well have recognised the voice of the kind of obsessive ranter who had helped her husband to an early grave, but she mustered an immediate, measured response (half the length of Mr Free's diatribe) in the very next issue of the magazine, of which a flavour must suffice:

> The origin of Settlements was very simple. A new sense of brotherhood, an awakened consciousness of our responsibility for the well-being of the community, some fuller knowledge of the conditions under which masses of the people live, made us keenly aware of the great gulf which separates east and west, of the almost immeasurable want of understanding between different sections of the community. To many it seemed that one way of drawing closer together would be for some of those who possessed means and leisure to go and live amongst the great working class population of the East End of London, so that they might learn to know them as neighbours, and as neighbours might help them to make their lives fuller and richer. Perhaps the whole movement owes its first inspiration to Edward Denison. But many others were eager to follow where he had pointed the way … at first in the east of London, afterwards in the south, and the north, and now slowly in those newly settled great areas of population in the far west … People rush down the Fulham Road in their motors to polo matches at Hurlingham, or to Hammersmith and the higher reaches of the river to see the Boat Race, or to Kew to enjoy the beautiful gardens. They remark upon how the houses have spread, and notice that all the market gardens have disappeared. But few stop to think of the people who are living in those countless rows of little houses, many of them still too new to be as yet blackened by the smoke of London, but yet no more fit to accommodate several families in one house than the old tenements in the East End. Here too a great population is living as separate as the east or the south from the wealthier inhabitants of London, if not quite as remote so far as distance is concerned. Here too it would seem that there is opening for the work of a Settlement … The most extravagant defender of the parson's freehold cannot wish to make it extend to the right to decide who shall live within his parish. But he is justified in claiming to control the Church work done in his parish, and the residents in a Church Settlement must be very careful to undertake no work in any parish where they are not wanted. The Head of the Settlement will never claim for the Settlement nor for its workers, as Mr Free asserts, 'independence of the parish priest,' nor will she demand that the residents should show 'exclusive allegiance' to her … Where the need is so great, there is room for service of many kinds. Nothing is so pitiable as that any time or energy should be wasted in contention. Each may surely find enough to do without pausing to attack or hinder others. [9]

***

"THE VERGE OF CIVILISATION"

> " ... on the eastern side, Fulham is unsatisfactory from whatever
> point of view it is regarded. It is one of the dumping grounds of
> London, and threatens to become a new criminal quarter."
>
> Charles Booth [1]

Miss Wickham, beginning her 1948 account of the first forty years of BCH's history, chose to quote from Fulham's great historian, Charles Fèret, whose *Fulham Old & New*, published in 1900, evoked a bucolic recent past:

> Until comparatively recent years Fulham has been an agricultural district, devoted mainly to the cultivation of vegetables, fruit and flowers. Orchards were very numerous, producing an abundance of strawberries, raspberries, currants, gooseberries, plums, pears and apples. Numbers of Shropshire girls would trudge to Fulham in the season to pick strawberries and convey them into London. About midnight these girls, often numbering upwards of a hundred, would walk with the large baskets, weighing some 40 lbs, on their heads, filled with punnets of strawberries, and singing a tune that gave them a step to march to. [2]

But those days were only a memory by the time the Creightons came to the Palace, so what now was the condition of Fulham, 'the verge of civilisation' [3] as Virginia Woolf called it? The last Visitation Returns during Mandell Creighton's time as Bishop of London, those for 1900, are preserved in Lambeth Palace Archives. The Rural Deanery of Fulham collected twenty-seven responses; the ministers were asked a range of questions - How large were their regular congregations? Did they run a Sunday School? Did they observe any particular rituals? But it is the last two questions on the forms that give us some insight into the problems church workers felt they faced:

What are the chief difficulties in the way of your Ministry?
"Poverty and indifference" "Indifference to religious influence" "Indifference" "General indifference and the worldliness of London life" "Indifference and the growing secularisation of the Lord's Day" "Indifference to everything except money making and pleasure getting and the most serious relaxation of parental control"

What is the general moral condition of your Parish?
"Drunkenness is very evident, especially on Saturdays" "I know of no brothels, but the moral tone is anything but good" "Vice is not openly organized, except in drink shops" "Reckless drinking, especially among the laundry women" "Intemperance is the besetting sin of the majority" "Betting and gambling are our prominent vices" "There is a great deal of drunkenness and disregard of the marriage tie" "Low moral condition owing to gambling and overdrinking" [4]

Limiting our survey only to Fulham reflects the way BCH developed its activities; although the Appeals and advance publicity spoke of work throughout the Rural

Deanery of Fulham, that is to say Hammersmith as well, in practice BCH rapidly came to confine itself to working in Fulham. Miss Harry, BCH secretary during World War II, admitted as much in a letter to lawyers discussing BCH's Constitution; "Actually the work definitely ceased in the parish of Hammersmith some long time ago." [5] It would not be until the two Metropolitan Boroughs united into the London Borough of Hammersmith in 1965 (subsequently renamed Hammersmith *and Fulham* in 1979, after prolonged complaints from aggrieved Fulhamites) that BCH began seriously to reach anywhere north of the Broadway.

Charles Booth, surveying the area at the turn of the twentieth century, conveyed in his introduction a sense of the 'remoteness' of Fulham:

> The true Fulham lies south of the District Railway line, a locality hardly less accessible than the corresponding loop of the river at the Isle of Dogs. Like the Isle of Dogs, it consists of low lying land encompassed by the river, but in the place of a fringe of streets and houses with docks and open space in the middle, we have here a central group of houses, with open fields still available for building (or for a public garden) stretching down to the banks of the Thames. These fields are now being rapidly built upon. Nowhere else within the London boundary north of the Thames has population increased in recent years so fast as here, and the movement continues … The twenty years from 1871 to 1891, and more particularly the last ten of these, mark the greatest period of Fulham's development. Within this time the population increased fourfold, and between 1881 and 1891 more than seven thousand working-class houses were erected in the parish. The census figures for 1901 show that the increase still continues, though at a much less rapid rate. [6]

The actual census figures for Fulham are worth noting: 1871, 23,378; 1881, 42,895 (+83%); 1891, 91,640 (+114%); 1901, 137,289 (+50%); 1911, 153,284 (+9%). The overall increase in forty years being 656%, which is a very rapid farewell to strawberries, gooseberries and apples, and a very rapid hello to poor drains, smelly basements and the loss of 'community' in the face of 'mass.'

Booth was quite taken with West Fulham, 'the buoyant tone is marked', he said. Talking of St Augustine's, the Rev[d] Propert's parish, he was impressed with the vigour of it all:

> Social questions come to the front, and again the boundaries of Church action are opened wide; art and music, literature and natural science are invoked, together with civic enthusiasm, in support of morality and religion. The inspiration from within has so far touched the outer world that money has been forthcoming, and now a large and beautiful church has sprung up alongside the mission hall. [7]

However, he went on, even in West Fulham there were some voices 'who spoke with less satisfaction of their work,'

> The instability arising from frequent removals, for instance, is greatly felt. Families shift to another and a fresher house, with as little hesitation as rooms are changed at an hotel. A new house is thought no more than a new suit of clothes. The change commonly involves a change of parish. This is regarded by one of the clergy as a chief cause of the lack of religious observance; while in another parish the people, though well spoken of, are thought to be difficult to reach for this same reason. The parochial tie is disregarded. Some, it is said, alternate

church with chapel going, while many others avoid religious obligation altogether. In these cases it would seem that the mark has not quite been hit by the churches. [8]

East Fulham, on the other hand, was plainly a cause for concern:

The bulk of the population is untouched, and special mission work among the poor is as usual very unsatisfactory. The working classes are indifferent, and the poor rough and not easy to deal with. There are also many prostitutes and loose women living here in St James's parish, a feature for which the exhibitions are blamed ... For rough poverty and crime, things become worse as we go further south, and reach their greatest depth in Langford Road. "Drunken, lazy, vicious, rough, as bad as any there used to be in the low streets off Drury Lane. The police must come in force if they want to take a man." "In a place like this it is seen that the worst are quite as bad as ever they were. If they are not the same men, they have the same names as the characters who made Parker Street (Drury Lane) notorious." So run our notes on this street. [9]

The apparent continuity between Drury Lane and Langford Road was a simple function of re-housing; the residents of Langford Road had been moved to Fulham when the courts around Drury Lane were being demolished. Booth also found grounds for disquiet around the Wandsworth Bridge Road:

Streets are fast springing into existence, and are occupied before the houses are dry, and while the roadway is still unmade. Not all the houses are badly built, nor are all the occupants of doubtful character, but many of them are: and this is so especially to the east side of the road and towards the river side. Here it is said that the people are poorer than they look. They make as good an outward show as they can, but live by their wits: "cheats, betting touts, forgers, and confidence trick men" are all to be found here. Thus, with houses badly built and badly tenanted, tenants coming and going and every change a change for the worse, we have here the beginning of a black area. [10]

Booth was appalled at the inadequate response of the municipal authorities:

Many hundreds of houses have been erected in a manner which never should have been allowed, and even now not all is done that might be to check the jerry builder ... The [Medical] Inspector [of the LCC], reporting in 1896 on the condition of the district, notes as a marked feature the inferior character of the building which has taken place in some parts, and states that houses only recently built had become defective, owing to the doubtful quality of the material used in their construction and to bad workmanship ... Over two-thirds of the houses visited by him were defective, and that there was in some instances considerable overcrowding ... The local Medical Officer amply confirms these statements ... He speaks of the jerry builder as "Fulham's worst trouble; it has a shocking lot of houses." [11]

This Fulham then, despite the undoubted charms of Fulham Palace, Bishops Park, All Saints and one or two other pockets of old-world style, was generally a rather mean landscape, and the people were sometimes struggling with particular problems arising from 'progress', as the 1912 BCH Annual Report pointed out, "Fulham has suffered much from the decline in the horse omnibus trade, and the many minor occupations dependent upon it, consequent on the introduction of the motor traffic." [12]

Addressing the Fulham and Hammersmith Charity Organisation Society at Fulham Palace on 1 February 1889, the great housing pioneer Octavia Hill laid out in the simplest terms what these circumstances required from those minded to help:

The man, or woman, or child is poor for some cause. Either he has got into some place where there is no need of the special power he has, out of the groove where his value would be marketable, and it wants sympathetic imaginative consideration to see to what he can be put, or he is worth no one's money; he is ill and needs cure, or he is idle, or ignorant, or bad tempered, and needs - my friends, what does he need? If any member of our own family or circle is at fault, has got crooked with himself or the world, is hopeless, or listless, or impatient, or incapable - do we find it easy to put things right? We must not help too much, or he becomes dependent; we must not help too little, or he loses hope; we spend in watchful, ever more continuous tenderness year after year, thankful if, after long seasons, we find him better ... I am quite awed when I think what our impatient charity is doing to the poor of London: men, who should hold up their heads as self-respecting fathers of families, learning to sing like beggars in the streets - all because we give them pennies ... Impatience seems to me the curse of the time; even our benevolence is in such frantic haste; we hurry even to *seem* to mend matters, and we make them tenfold worse, and some of us hardly care. [13]

***

- 5 -

"WORK WAS AT ONCE BEGUN"

"Fear not to sow because of the birds."
Robert Browning [1]

By the autumn of 1908 Miss Wickham and the first seven residents were hard at work. Whatever the attitude of the Rev[d] Free at St Clement's, there were calls for help from eight neighbouring parishes, and BCH women were involved in clubs, district visiting, Sunday Schools and Bands of Hope. Assistance was also being given to the local COS offices, four Children's Care Committees, the Fulham Apprenticeship and Skilled Employment Committee, the Invalid Children's Aid Association, the Children's Country Holiday Fund and the School for Mothers. This last, at 92 Greyhound Road, was known as the 'Babies' Welcome' and was virtually an annexe of BCH. The first Annual Report noted, "Care is taken to give to the different residents such help in their work and such further training as they may need, and they have attended lectures on various social and philanthropic subjects." [2]

By the time of the second Annual Report, BCH had expanded its activities, in addition to all the above, to include visiting patients in the consumption ward at Fulham Hospital, home visiting for patients of the Margaret Street Consumption Hospital, help to Miss Arnould's Association for the Physically and Mentally Defective, assistance at the Fulham Refuge, close co-operation with the District Nursing Association and representation on the committees of several organisations, both local and metropolitan, including the Employment Association for the Defective, the Research Branch of the Christian Social Union, the management of two groups of LCC schools and the Metropolitan Association for Befriending Young Servants.

There were also, during the winter months, regular monthly 'At Homes', hosted by Mrs Creighton and Miss Wickham, to which all BCH Associates and residents were invited, at which topics such as 'Health Visiting', 'Girls' Clubs', 'Study Circles', 'The work of the MABYS' and 'The Personal Service Association' were discussed.

During the first three years of BCH's life, a reduced rent of £75 per annum was paid to the landlord [the Freehold was not purchased until 1953] in recognition of the need for extensive repairs, but from the start of 1911 the full payment, £115, was required. The Annual Report for 1910 laid out the situation for subscribers and associates in what was the first of an annually recurring series of new ways of asking for more money:
> The first three years have now expired and the larger amount will have to be found. It must also be remembered that with every fresh year of wear and tear more money will have to be spent upon repairs. This year, for instance, it will be necessary to repaint the front of the house. BCH is in a very open position and the sun streams full upon it, which is pleasant enough for the residents, but

comes hard on the paint. The total cash receipts for 1910 amounted to £409-18-11, and the expenditure for 1911 is estimated at about £450. As at any time a sudden emergency may arise and necessitate an unexpected expenditure in repairing the house, the Committee would be very glad to be able to put aside the present balance, or some part of it, to meet such an emergency. This can only be done if there is an increase in the yearly income. Far from being content with the present state of things, therefore, the Committee asks new subscribers and associates to come forward in order to place the financial affairs of the Settlement on a thoroughly sound basis. [3]

Pausing for a moment to consider the premises Mrs Creighton had chosen; they had begun life as Numbers 1-4 Emily Terrace, the freehold held by a Baron Barreto [4] who granted a 99 year lease.

LBHF Archives

A view down Lillie Road from the junction with Fulham Palace Road.
Taken 1893-4, it shows the road not yet made up.
On the right are the railings of the recreation ground,
on the left the bulk of Everington Road Board School.
The block with the advertisement ('Batey & Co A1 non-alcoholic Pale Ale')
on its end wall is Emily Terrace, built 1881,
which would in 1908 be taken over as Bishop Creighton House.

33

Mrs Creighton took over the lease in December 1907. Some time in the preceding twenty years the house numbering system had been regularised and Emily Terrace became Numbers 374-380 Lillie Road. Thrown up as they were during Fulham's jerry-building bonanza, when drainage and other municipal services often struggled to keep up with the boom, they have never in the fullest sense been 'fit for purpose' and over these last hundred years the thought has several times arisen of knocking them down and rebuilding with BCH's requirements incorporated from the start. The basement has flooded regularly; June 1916, January 1919, September 1921, July 1927, January 1940, May 1954, March 1970, May 1979, March 1985, August 2004 and July 2007. At a Council Meeting on 2 November 1927 it was minuted, with a hint of despair, "An estimate has been received for the fitting of an anti-flooding valve in the basement at a cost of approx. £30. On asking the advice of the architect, Mr Wood stated that the success of the valve could not be guaranteed. He believed that negotiations were in progress with the LCC to provide relief sewer accommodation for Fulham which would remedy the flooding." [5] After the 1954 flooding, when it was laconically observed, "the drains could not cope with the sudden downpour," the Council noted on 7 July that, "A letter was received from the Borough Surveyor saying that the flood was most unusual and unlikely to happen again." [6] And, as if flooding wasn't enough, the basement has also had repeated outbreaks of dry rot; July 1921, September 1943, July 1944, July 1946, January 1948, December 1955, September 1990 and November 1995.

What makes this litany of maintenance problems the more surprising is the list of architects who have been involved with BCH from the start. The first architects' drawings of the premises come from the offices of the distinguished partnership of Arnold Dunbar Smith and Cecil Brewer, who are best-remembered in this connection for their design of the University Hall Settlement (1895-7), now Mary Ward House, in Tavistock Place. Described by Nikolaus Pevsner as 'one of the most charming pieces of architecture designed at the time in England,' [7] this was of course their design from scratch, whereas at BCH they were adapting, patching and knocking through. Their two sets of drawings for BCH, dated December 1907 and January 1908 [8], show considerable pencilled alterations, suggesting the actuality of three not-very-well-built-in-the-first-place houses in the end defeated their attempts at originality. Subsequent architects who have been involved with BCH - Edwin Wood, Albert Cowtan, Arthur Moberly (of Slater, Moberly & Uren), Picozzi & Partners, Support Community Building Design and, most recently, Simon Humphreys, have all laboured against the basic intractability of the existing rabbit warren. Thus, when, in the last ten years, thoughts turned to achieving disabled access to all floors, it was simple enough to plan where a lift might be grafted on to the rear elevation, but then realised that all the doors and corridors on the 1st and 2nd floors are unfortunately too narrow for wheelchair manoeuvres.

But, against this tale of woe must be set one hundred years of successful compromise, of a building that, although it must have perennially infuriated its inhabitants, has served several generations on this spot so that it is now loved, and known, where it is for what it is; homely, human and welcoming.

One piece of knocking-through preceded the arrival of BCH by some years: since the 1890s the ground floor of Numbers 374 and 376 had been occupied by the Lillie Road

Girls' Club, who had taken down the party wall to create the space that is still the main hall today. The origins of this club are lost but an intriguing glimpse was offered by a supporter in sending her subscription for 1932: she said she had helped to found the club 'over fifty years ago' and that it had first been based at Star Road Board School as a club for laundry girls, before moving to Lillie Road. [9] In 1914 the club would become a fully-integrated part of BCH, and in 1916 change its name to the Creighton House Club.

A significant addition to BCH's support network came in 1911 with the affiliation of three schools to the Settlement: North Foreland Lodge, Hertfordshire, Downe House, Kent and Belstead House in Suffolk all decided that their girls would collect money each term to support the work of the Settlement. In years to come they would welcome parties on outings from BCH, until Downe House moved from Kent and broke the connection, and Belstead House closed down in 1940. But the annual 'Daffodil Day' trip to North Foreland Lodge continued almost for a century until the school closed four years ago, and was an event recalled with something like awe by many BCH Club members: each personally looked after by two schoolgirls during the visit and royally entertained with copious cream teas, they were sent home at the end of the day with as many daffodils as they cared to carry.

BCH

35

1911 also saw the decoration of the hall at BCH with murals in egg tempera by Henry Tonks of the Slade School of Art and half a dozen of his pupils, including Dora Carrington, Elsie McNaught, H. F. Garret and William Roberts. Tonks was keen to get his students engaged and interested in mural painting, and BCH was happy to give him the walls to work on. It was noted in BCH Council minutes in 1923[10] that the murals already needed some restoration, and when BCH was bombed during the blitz in 1940 they were further damaged and the decision was reluctantly taken to paint over them. The possibility of restoration has been recently considered but rejected on the grounds that a great deal of expensive expertise might be deployed to uncover nothing very much. So all that remains to pique our interest is this preliminary pencil and ink drawing, 49.5 x 34.3cm, by William Roberts, called 'Carpenters At Work: study for mural at Bishop Creighton House.'

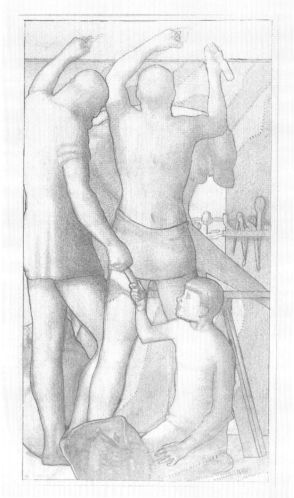

Courtesy Whitworth Art Gallery

36

There is also the rather ghostly faded sepia photo below, taken some time during the 1920s, where, behind the unknown smiling girl in the foreground, one can just make out something of the murals on the end wall of the hall:

BCH

...

1911 also saw the birth of a Fulham branch of the Workers' Education Association and, probably because of a personal friendship between Miss Wickham and the founder, Albert Mansbridge, BCH hosted the inaugural meeting and Miss Wickham took on the task of being treasurer. This brought BCH into useful contact with the local leaders of the Labour movement, and Miss Wickham long after recalled an outing with them:

> A Whit Monday still stands out in the memory of one of them (then an ardent young man with a very red tie, pale and wan from underpaid long hours in an underground bakery). It was spent at Oxford seeing colleges and the Eights from a College barge, with tea at Canon Scott Holland's Christ Church garden where the party listened spellbound to his brilliant talk. [11]

Most of the few papers, reports and other documents that survive from this period give us little of that human detail, and we are largely left to wonder at what went on, but occasionally a cameo comes through, as in this report on hospital visiting:

> A few special visits have been undertaken for hospital almoners. Miss Macey visited a young man who was rebellious against the doctor's orders to keep on his back, and by giving him lessons in French, which he was anxious to learn, helped to keep him contented until he recovered his health. [12]

BCH's rapid rise to prominence, not only locally but also across the metropolis, was recognized in November 1910 when it was chosen as the location for the first ever conference of the Federation of Women's Settlements, attended by the Heads and other representatives of nearly all the London Settlements. No record survives of what was discussed, but Miss Wickham could note in the Annual Report, "It is a great help to a new Settlement to be associated with those who in other parts of London have done so much to raise and brighten the lives of their neighbours, and to train and inspire social workers." [13]

BCH's early years coincided with a time of significant progressive social legislation, on a scale beyond all precedent, under the last Liberal government of 1905 to 1915, which was aimed, said Henry Campbell-Bannerman, at making Britain "less of a pleasure ground for the few and more of a treasure house for the nation." [14] While successive budgets shifted more taxation onto the rich, measures regarding the feeding and medical inspection of schoolchildren, workmen's compensation, sweated industries, non-contributory old age pensions, health insurance and labour exchanges brought wholesale change to the social landscape, and incidentally gave encouragement to the kind of campaigns that bodies like BCH were taking up.

Fulham had an uncommonly high rate of infant mortality, 116 per 1000, and BCH took the lead locally in the arguments for maternity and infant welfare, which led to the setting-up of the 'School for Mothers' in Greyhound Road, only the second to be opened in London. This was a typical example of the process whereby a facility was first brought into existence with voluntary workers, gradually seen to be of value by the municipal or metropolitan authorities, given support by them, and then finally taken over by them - a sequence repeated with several of BCH's brainchilds over the years. It was for example at BCH that the first Children's Care Committees in West London were set up; based at individual schools, these committees concerned themselves with the deprived, maladjusted or sometimes simply lonely, unhappy children in the school, visited their homes, counselled parents, advised on medical treatment, and perhaps recommended them to the Children's Country Holiday Fund. The 1912 Annual Report noted how this field was expanding:

> We are now sending workers to four or five of the Care Committees in the neighbourhood. There seems to be literally no end to the number of helpers who these Committees can absorb. On all sides we hear of the same need for more visitors to follow up the medical inspection of the children, to advise the parents about their after-care when they leave school, and to assist in putting them into good trades, in connection with the work of the Apprenticeship Committees and of the Labour Exchanges. The work is extraordinarily varied, and full of human interest, and it is much to be hoped that more people will be found willing to take it up. [15]

The 1913 Annual Report gave more detail of the kind of human interest this work involved:

> A delicate, very nervous boy, who was brought to our notice by the District Nurses; he was invited to come and learn something of gardening under Miss Falkner in our small back garden and this has been a great delight to him.
> A family, three of whom were afflicted by paralysis and partial blindness

which it was assumed must inevitably get worse. Special treatment has been obtained for the youngest of the three, aged 16, which has improved his sight and general powers and it is hoped he may soon be able to do light work in the country and in time become self-supporting. The elder sister and brother have been given new interests through being sent away to the country for part of the summer. In the case of the sister who was much too crippled to travel in the ordinary way the family shared in the delight of driving to Woking in a motor car lent through the kind interest of one of our day workers…

An anonymous donation of £5 sent to BCH to be spent on 'giving a holiday to tired women' was handed on to Miss Williams, Superintendent of the Fulham School for Mothers. She despatched three mothers and their babies to the sea-side for a fortnight and wrote afterwards, "When asked if they would like a holiday the answer was 'Why yes, but there's no chance.' I told them that a friend had thought of them and would like them to go, and their joy was worth seeing. They went away looking and feeling very tired and returned different beings. I only wish our friend could have seen the change brought about by her kindness."

The work of following up Medical Inspection has been greatly helped by the new local treatment centres which are much more satisfactory than out-patient departments of distant hospitals. In one very poor school where there were special difficulties to be overcome the proportion of children examined during the year whose parents had been persuaded to carry out the doctor's orders was 75 per cent, which is certainly a great improvement. [16]

Now, a century later, all that work has been absorbed into borough, metropolitan or NHS bureaucracy, and it is difficult to conceive of a time when such things depended only and simply on committed Christian volunteers. Equally of another era is the report of BCH volunteers carrying out research in Fulham, on behalf of a Home Office Committee, into conditions of labour among van boys:

Much interesting information was collected. It is much to be hoped that some improvement will be effected in the condition of the work of the van boys, and in the terribly long hours which are expected from them. BCH has also co-operated with the Research Committee of the Christian Social Union in various enquiries into industrial conditions. [17]

These earliest years were also BCH's most Christian years; parish work occupied a 'foremost place' in BCH activities and volunteers involved in teaching at Sunday Schools were coached by a series of lectures laid on by the Bishop's Sunday School Council. In fact so many were the demands for help from different parishes in the Rural Deanery that the Annual Reports had to regret that not all of them could be satisfied. That gradual process of secularisation which would begin in the 1920s was still in an undreamt of future; in the Edwardian years bishops still came regularly to hold services in the chapel, Holy Communion was celebrated once a month, BCH Council Meetings and At Homes began or ended with prayers, and the lectures and study courses laid on for the residents were overwhelmingly on religious topics, or brought a religious perspective to a subject. The At Homes for Associates, which were graced by distinguished speakers such as Lord Grey of Falloden, Canon Scott Holland, Bishop Gore, Margaret Bondfield, Albert Mansbridge, William Temple and Lady Frances Balfour, ranged over subjects such as 'The Workers' Education Association', 'Schools for Mothers', 'Apprenticeships', 'Girls' Clubs', 'Sunday School Kindergartens',

'The Campaign against Tuberculosis', 'District Visiting', 'Labour Exchanges for Women', 'Social Work in America', 'The National Women's Labour League', 'Women and the Insurance Act' and 'The Need for Thoroughness in Charitable Work'. Lady Frederick Cavendish, an old friend of Mrs Creighton, led a meeting about the White Slave Traffic and, after a trip across the Atlantic, Mrs Creighton hosted an At Home centred on her 'Impressions of Canada.'

BISHOP CREIGHTON HOUSE,
378, LILLIE ROAD, FULHAM, S.W.6.
Station—Hammersmith

Mrs. CREIGHTON & Miss WICKHAM
AT HOME TO ASSOCIATES
THURSDAY, JANUARY 24TH,
WEDNESDAY, FEBRUARY 27TH
& THURSDAY, MARCH 20TH.

SUBJECTS:

TEA, 4 P M	Jan. 24th "Women's Auxiliary Service" Speaker—COMMANDANT MARY ALLEN.
CONFERENCE, 4.30	Feb. 27th "London Parks" Speaker—LADY TRUSTRAM EVE.
CHAPEL, 5.15.	Mar. 20th "The Christian Student Movement" Speaker—W. A. G. PITE, Esq. Asst. Sec.

BISHOP CREIGHTON HOUSE,
378, LILLIE ROAD, FULHAM, S.W.   (Station: Hammersmith)

Buses 11, 30, 74 pass the door.

A LECTURE WILL BE GIVEN BY
REV. J. C. PRINGLE
on
ST. FRANCIS OF ASSISI
on
FRIDAY, DECEMBER 3RD AT 6 P.M.

There will be a collection on behalf of Stepney Skilled Employment Association.

Typical BCH printed ephemera of the early days.

40

Associates were encouraged to feel themselves members of a club and their membership cards reminded them of their commitment:

Associates are subscribers who undertake to show their definite personal interest in the work of the Settlement in one or more of the following ways.

1. By remembering BISHOP CREIGHTON HOUSE — in their prayers.

2. By staying at the Settlement or coming on one or more days in the week to help in the work.

3. By coming to Settlement gatherings and social evenings to meet other associates, neighbours and club members.

4. (a) By sending country produce, Hospital and Convalescent Home letters ; toys, books and clothes for children ; books and periodicals for libraries.

(b) By trying to interest friends in the Settlement and its needs, and by getting new subscribers and donors.

The charge for board and residence at Bishop Creighton House is 35/- a week. Proportionate charges for single nights and for meals.

All subscribers of 2/6 upwards have the right to vote at the annual election of the Council and to receive the annual report.

But even in this seemingly idyllic Edwardian launch phase of BCH's life, events could sometimes introduce a sombre note: In 1911 a Study Circle on English Church History, arranged at BCH in association with the Church Reading Union, was steered by 'inspiring' talks from a Mrs Carter. Unfortunately, however, the full programme could not be completed after Mrs Carter went down with the *Titanic*.

***

"KEEP THE HOME FIRES BURNING"

"Even things which might, in these terrible days, be at first sight
called luxuries, such as schemes for the happiness and health of
children, come under the appeal of 'Keep the Home Fires Burning,'
and in the case of some work, for example, the preservation of
infant life, there is a newly widespread recognition that it is an
urgent National need."

BCH Annual Report, 1915 [1]

Although the war drums had been pounding over Europe for some months before
World War One broke out, there were considerable hopes in Britain that it would be a
'European war' and that we could somehow stand to one side. That certainly had been
the thrust behind the policy of Lord Grey of Falloden, the Creightons' old friend, now
British Foreign Secretary, but it was in the end impossible to avoid engagement and on
4 August 1914 Britain went to war with Germany.

Most immediately, as far as BCH was concerned, the war meant the recall of parties of
children from various holiday destinations and the cancellation of holidays that had
been booked for later that summer. Also, as a side-effect of the initial flurry of patriotic
volunteering among the men of Fulham, there was a huge amount of counselling and
visiting to be done among wives and other dependents while the organisation of the
Soldiers' and Sailors' Families Association pulled itself together; one early product of
this was BCH's first women's club, open every day, for the wives of men serving in the
forces. There was also, in the first flush of 'patriotism', an ugly outbreak of mob
violence against German shops and restaurants, and BCH allied itself with a long-
established organisation, the Friends of Foreigners in Distress, to alleviate the situation
especially of elderly and isolated German women who had not been interned. The
1914 Annual Report evoked the anguish this work touched upon:

The Settlement undertook to act as Almoner for the [Friends of Foreigners
in Distress] war cases in Fulham. These are mostly to do with the families of
Germans or Austrians thrown suddenly out of good and regular work, their
wives and children being in nearly all cases English by birth. To those who
have near relations fighting on both sides the tragedy of the War comes
specially close and these people have been intensely grateful for any friendliness
shown them. [2]

Another effect of the War was abruptly to throw large numbers of British people in
various occupations out of work, and nationally the Prince of Wales' Fund was set up
to deal with this. In Fulham the Fund was administered by an Executive Committee set
up by the Mayor, and predictably Miss Wickham was invited to be on it. There was a
good deal of visiting, particularly in connection with 'Queen Mary's Workroom,' a
make-work scheme for the large number of dressmakers out of work, which was

managed by the Women's Sub-Committee of the Mayor's Committee. The Local Government Board additionally involved BCH workers in research into the war's effects on a range of occupations, particularly the 'home workers' in the borough.

A curious footnote about the First World War, worth mentioning in passing, is that in all writing at the time it was referred to as 'the War', with a capital W, whereas the Second World War would only be 'the war.' What this signifies is for others to determine. Although the War dominated life and work at BCH, there was a determined effort to keep up as much as possible of the normal strands of Settlement life; the Lillie Road Girls' Club, now integrated into BCH (and shortly to change its name to the Creighton House Club), maintained a full programme; the 'Seniors' and 'Juniors' having separate evenings for recreation and dancing, and joint sessions for classes with the LCC providing teachers for drill, dressmaking and millinery. BCH also ran, once a week, a Guild of Play for very poor children which was managed by students from the Fulham LCC Training College (this unfortunately came to an end, for reasons out of BCH's hands, when the LCC moved the Training College to South London and the students were no longer available). And of course a full calendar of conferences and At Homes was arranged, with such topics as 'Women in Local Government' (keynote speaker the Duchess of Marlborough), 'Girl Guides', 'Schemes for Training Church Workers', 'Women Police' and 'Why the Church does not Appeal to Young Women'.

By the second year of the War, after the initial dust had settled, some of the work of BCH's residents and day workers had changed; some of the special agencies set up for the relief of distress in the first phase had become largely redundant; women and girls, instead of the half-crowns they had been handed as alms, were now achieving a certain independence and replacing men across a range of occupations from bus driving and conducting to munitions work. The work among 'distressed foreigners' had dwindled to visiting a few elderly German women; the men having being interned, their families were either returned to Germany or relieved through the Board of Guardians. The 1915 Annual Report explained a change in the work involved in the Soldiers' and Sailors' Families Association:

> Visiting for the SSFA continues, and though much of the need for material help has passed, the need for friendship and sympathy, as well as for advice as to saving etc, is greater than ever. This does not mean that our workers endorse the sweeping accusations often made against 'soldiers' wives.'
> We have been glad to testify to the increasing comfort and care of children in many poor homes, and to the splendidly brave and patriotic spirit of the great majority of the women. The few cases of serious drinking with which we have been concerned have been of women known to drink before the War. [3]

Perhaps the biggest change in the neighbourhood came at Easter 1915, when the Fulham Workhouse and Infirmary was converted into a Military Hospital. BCH had been involved in visiting there before the War, but now found even greater opportunities to help out. Miss Batt of BCH, besides maintaining contact with her former clients, the consumption patients, who had been farmed out to other institutions, now concerned herself more or less full-time with the soldier patients' welfare and, for example, worked hard getting weekly invitations to tea and drives for those who were mobile. Miss Kingsford of BCH became the hospital's Hon Librarian,

43

circulating books and magazines and of course soliciting donations of suitable reading matter from BCH Associates. BCH also organised hymn singing in the wards on Sundays, which was described as very welcome since no services were held in the wards for those unable to get to the hospital chapel.

BCH

Senior nursing staff at Fulham Military Hospital, 1918.
Lieutenant-Colonel Parsons RAMC (front row centre).
Miss Wickham (back row centre).

By far the greatest service BCH rendered to the hospital was the work of another Miss Wickham, the younger sister of the Warden. The Warden, Catherine, was of course always referred to simply as Miss Wickham, and her sister was distinguished from her by being called Miss C. Wickham, in her case 'C' for Christian; it remains one of the curious mysteries of BCH's records, up to and including the obituaries of both ladies, that the fact they were sisters is never referred to. Miss Christian Wickham was never a resident at BCH, always a day worker, travelling from her home in Kensington, but her contribution, begun during the first War, was to continue almost until the second war. Her skill was in therapeutic massage; in peacetime she would apply her touch to young children, but during the War it was wounded soldiers who benefited. This testimonial letter from the Commandant of the hospital, Lieutenant-Colonel Parsons, written at the end of the War, makes clear the value of her work:

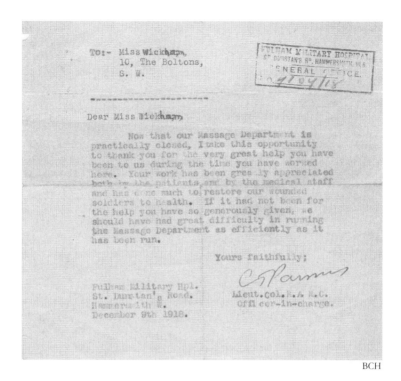

BCH

It should not be thought that the War stopped all normal activities; life continued at BCH in many ways undisturbed; the residents paid 25/- a week for their board and lodging, and Associates could always turn up for a meal, and a bed if available. The prices to them were b&b 2/6, lunch 9d, tea 6d, supper 1/-. On 11 April 1916 the Executive Committee, in one of the earliest minutes still extant, decided to raise the housekeeper's wages in July and, as a mark of esteem, give her a donation of £1 towards a new set of teeth.

The Girls' Club flourished throughout the War and towards the end achieved renown beyond the borough, as the Annual Report boasted:

The chief event of 1918 was the distinction won at the NOGC [National Organisation of Girls' Clubs] Display at the Old Vic Theatre. Both Seniors and Juniors gave performances of country dancing, and their ambulance work was a cause of special interest to Princess Mary, who was the guest of honour. As members of the Old Vic Shakespeare Society they acted the trial Scene from *Henry VIII* and this was chosen by Mr Ben Greet and the other judges for special praise, and the Club was given a beautiful edition of Shakespeare as a trophy. They have since been asked to act the same scene to clubs in various parts of London. [4]

By the time of this Report, BCH was quite stretched; some workers had been called away for war work elsewhere, and the Settlement was short of bodies, equally there were 'new calls for work brought both by the stress of War and by the dawning of Peace.'

Additionally, and not for the last time, the Treasurer drew the attention of the BCH Council to the 'very serious state of affairs' regarding the Settlement's finances; subscriptions and donations had fallen gradually every year since the first fine flush of 1908, and at the same time, BCH had been expanding its activities into new fields - it was, for example, represented on no less than forty committees, and doing some kind of work in connection with the majority of them. The line between solvency and collapse was to remain a slim one for most of the decades ahead and it is indicative of a certain kind of all-hands-to-the-wheel mentality that when, at an Executive Committee Meeting on 13 January 1919, there was mention of Miss Stapleton, a prospective new resident, Miss Wickham suggested, "If she comes it would be a convenience if she could bring some of her own furniture." [5]

***

"THE DESIGN OF THE INSTITUTION SHALL BE..."

"I am sure it is important that the Constitution should make it
plain that Bishop Creighton House is an Anglican foundation.
These things can be assumed by those who know and then forgotten
by subsequent generations."

The Bishop of Kensington [1]

At a meeting of the BCH Executive Committee on 12 October 1920, the Treasurer, Miss Curtis, reported that she had not yet had a reply to her letter to the Collector of Taxes in Fulham requesting an abatement of Income Tax. Then at a Council meeting on 4 April 1921, she reported that the authorities had replied and were refusing to grant BCH exemption from tax on the grounds of its charitable work. At another Executive Committee meeting on 3 October 1921, Mrs Hudson-Lyall said she had successfully claimed tax exemption for the Mothers' Union for several years on the grounds that it was a 'charitable society.' At the next Council meeting on 12 October 1921, Miss Synge undertook to enquire of St Hilda's East Settlement what they did about tax. Then, at the next Executive Committee meeting, on 7 November 1921, it was reported that Coutts Bank had felt unable to offer an opinion on the tax question without sight of the BCH 'Trust Deeds.' And finally, at an Executive Committee meeting on 18 January 1922, it was realised that nothing could be done about Income Tax "owing to the fact that no Trust Deed of the Settlement existed." At last therefore, at the next Council meeting, on 26 January 1922, Mrs Creighton said she would get her solicitors to draw up a Trust Deed - a formal legal statement of BCH's aims, organisational structure and rules - a mere fourteen years after the Settlement had come into existence. [2]

This Deed, duly signed by Mrs Creighton, dated 1 June 1922, was successful with the tax people, but was to cause some anguish over the coming decades. Its main clauses, after a good deal of legal preamble along the lines of 'To all whom the Presents shall come,' stated:

1. The Institution shall be called Bishop Creighton House.
2. The design of the Institution shall be as follows:
    a. To provide a Settlement or Social Welfare Centre for the benefit of the poor of the Parishes of Fulham and Hammersmith in the County of London and the surrounding districts with a view to facilitating and encouraging co-operation among neighbours and inhabitants of those

districts for the enrichment of social life and for furtherance of education.

    b. To assist the Local Authorities in any matters relating to the improvement of social conditions in the aforesaid districts by carrying on Welfare Centres, Public Dispensaries, Clinics and otherwise howsoever and providing accommodation therefore.

    c. To provide reading and recreation rooms, libraries, lecture classes and entertainments, working-girls' clubs, welfare clubs, a hostel for social workers and other facilities for any of the purposes aforesaid.

    d. By any of the means aforesaid, or by any other means that may be found expedient, to reform and improve the conditions of life among the inhabitants of the said districts. [3]

The Deed passed *nem con* through the next Council meeting without any discussion and it was only later, in the thirties, again in the forties, and again in the fifties that the Trustees sought to correct a serious flaw that no-one had noticed in the twenties: to wit, nowhere in the outline of BCH's purposes was there any mention of the Settlement's religious basis. The omission arose because at the time it was simply understood by all that *of course* BCH was an Anglican organisation, *of course* the Warden and residents were members of the Church of England and *of course* there would always be a Chapel at BCH. As Miss Wickham put it in a memorandum when, years later, there was agitation for a re-statement of BCH's aims, 'The Settlement was founded for social service *in the name of the Church*.' [4]

O God, make the door of this house wide enough
to receive all who need human love and fellowship;
narrow enough to shut out all envy, pride and strife.
Make its threshold smooth enough to be no stumbling
block to children, nor to straying feet, but rugged
and strong enough to turn back the tempter's power.

O God, make the door of this house a gateway
           to Thine Eternal Kingdom.

A prayer composed specially for Bishop Creighton House.
The author is unknown.

It was of course against a background of rising secularisation that the BCH Trustees sought to strengthen the Constitution by amending the 'design' to underscore the Settlement's religious basis. In the 1938 Annual Report, Miss Baber, BCH's second Warden, agonized at length:

It has been said by responsible people that the Christian Church is now in the position of a minority movement in a pagan world, that we are in fact back in the position of the early Church, unable to control the situation in which we find ourselves, but faced with the desperate urgency for missionary endeavour, and with the problem of how we are to permeate secular institutions with the Christian ethic. And this situation is felt acutely in miniature in the life and work of a Church Settlement. We find ourselves in close contact all day long with people who are frankly indifferent if not hostile to religion, and it is very difficult to know how to attack this situation. To attack it direct is perhaps to antagonize, and it takes a great deal of faith to go on believing that the daily routine of social work, undertaken by people who base their endeavours on Christian principles, is in the long run a powerful witness to the Truth. It is therefore vitally important that the people who now come to work in a Settlement such as ours, should be people who are definitely conscious of their vocation, and who can hold that to give is better than to receive in face of the increasing belief of the world about them, that to get all you can for as little as you can is the mark of the sensible man or woman. [5]

Later, Miss Marjorie Harry, the Bishop of London's secretary, who doubled as BCH secretary during World War Two, wrote to BCH's solicitors:
We should like to suggest an alteration in the first 'object.' What we had in mind was to alter Clause 2(a) to something like the following:-
"To provide a centre for religious, social and educational purposes among the people of the Deanery of Fulham and the surrounding districts, and if desirable in other areas, with a view to facilitating and encouraging co-operation among neighbours and inhabitants of those districts for their mutual enrichment.
However, she worried that there might be a catch:
In Clause 31 you will notice there is a proviso forbidding the alteration of any rule which alters or affects the design of the Institution. Does that mean that it is impossible to alter the wording of one of the 'objects'? [6]
Mr Pollard in reply had no doubts:
It is quite clear to me that Clause 31 of the Constitution prevents you making any change in Clause 2 … If you were to purport to make the alteration it would be void and it is probable that the Attorney General, the Trustees or any subscribers could obtain an injunction in Court restraining you from carrying the alteration into effect. [7]

Nonetheless, the desire to make BCH's Christian foundations explicit remained undimmed. The 44th Annual Report, for 1951-52, put it this way:
A Welfare State provides so much that the Settlement is needed to encourage personal resource and responsibility and independent judgment. More important than all, amid shattered faith and indifference to things of the Spirit, the Settlement holds fast the belief that man cannot live by bread alone in a world where he learns the bitter lesson that bread may all too easily become stones. So at the end of another year's work we say with St Thomas à Kempis…
Without the Way there is no going,
Without the truth there is no knowing,
Without the Life there is no living. [8]

That year Miss Wickham, reporting back to BCH Council from a meeting of the Diocesan Settlements Committee, said the question had been discussed and it was agreed that, "As the Constitution of other Settlements besides BCH had been drawn up when their religious basis had been taken for granted, it was thought important that they should now be safeguarded." [9]

Later in the fifties the matter was addressed again, and on 7 November 1956 the Council set up a sub-committee to explore the possibility of drawing up a codicil to the Constitution concerning the religious basis of the Settlement. The Bishop of Kensington, among others, was consulted, and finally a motion, drafted by the sub-committee and amended by the Bishop, *adding* to the Constitution rather than *altering* it, was put, as the sole item on the agenda, to a Special Subscribers' Meeting on 13 June 1957:

> While Bishop Creighton House, as a Settlement, must continue as a centre of co-operation between all people of goodwill - setting up no barriers as to its council or members - its religious basis shall be safeguarded and its traditions upheld by laying it down that:-
> (1) The Warden shall, as in the past, be a Communicant member of the Anglican Church and residents in responsible positions shall also be Anglicans, save in exceptional cases requiring the consent of the Council.
> (2) There shall always be a Chapel set apart for Prayers and Worship and for Services according to the rites of the Church of England. [10]

This was passed unanimously, and thus, after almost fifty years of existence during which BCH's work had been carried out by people invariably motivated by deep religious conviction, the religious basis was made statutory, just about at the time when Christianity was ceasing to be the driving force for many of the people signing up to be part of the BCH team.

When, forty years further on, for reasons to do with grant mechanisms, business accountability, and simply the different world of the late twentieth century, BCH became a Private Limited Company on 1 April 1997, the newly-formulated 'objects' would be wholly secular:

> (a) To provide a centre for the benefit of the inhabitants of the London Borough of Hammersmith and Fulham and surrounding area with a view to the provision of facilities in the interests of social welfare, advancement of education, leisure time occupation, community participation and improving the quality of life of said inhabitants.
> (b) To assist the Local Authorities in any matters relating to the improvement of social conditions.
> (c) To carry out any such charitable activities in furtherance of the aforementioned objectives.

***

Arthur Foley Winnington-Ingram
Bishop of London 1901-1939

VIGILANCE

"... the need has been lately felt for arousing public opinion
as to dangerous moral conditions in our streets and open spaces."
BCH Annual Report 1923 [1]

It will be recalled that one of Mrs Creighton's special concerns had long been the 'purity' campaign. She and her husband were involved in setting up the Council for the Promotion of Public Morality in London in 1900, and she had earlier been active on the Charing Cross Vigilance and Rescue Committee, which concerned itself with that particular moral black spot. As President of the Women's Patrol Committee of the National Union of Working Women she continued to be engaged in this work throughout the War. In 1917, Mrs Creighton put to the BCH Council that "she hoped the Club Committee would consider very carefully what this Club could do to help the patrols that were going to be started in Hammersmith." [2] Later, in the immediate aftermath of the War, it was felt there was a renewed need for special vigilance; in some ways, women had been 'liberated' by the War, and there was concern that liberty could too easily degenerate into dissipation. At the same time ideas of revolution were in the air and many demobbed soldiers were unimpressed with the peace they had come home to. Juvenile delinquency was another post-war problem, especially among the young who had lacked parental control during the War. These anxieties coalesced round three causes for concern; immorality, drinking and betting. The 1923 Annual Report elaborated:

> We have taken an active part during the past winter in the formation of Vigilance Committees, both in Fulham and in Hammersmith, and we were glad to welcome Miss Croxford, of the Women's Auxiliary Service, as a resident in connection with the work of these two committees. An urgent need also exists for some machinery for building up a public Conscience in the matter of betting, so disastrously prevalent among men, women and children, and especially for strengthening the hands of girls in factories and workshops against the inducements daily pressed on them, often in the name of 'charity.' Information on the subject has been accumulated, and we hope the moment may soon be ripe for some definite action. [3]

And the next year's Annual Report was similarly buoyant:

> Great things have been happening in the work begun here nearly two years ago, in the hope of giving protection to our growing boys and girls from the temptations of the streets. The small 'Vigilance' Committee after meeting in the Fulham Council Chamber was reinforced by a more widely representative body of people, and the patrolling of streets and open spaces is now carried on with the full approval and support of the local Police Force. Our own close connection with the work continues, as Mrs Orton, the organizing secretary, is living at BCH, Miss Anley is one of the trained patrols, and Miss Wickham is still acting as hon. secretary. [4]

Later in the same pages, the Creighton House Club spelled out their contribution:

Case after case shows itself of the wrong uses made of the complete freedom allowed in most of the poorest homes to the growing indolescent [sic]; of the double lives lived by so many pitiably young girls, well-behaved and well-dressed on the surface, and seemingly not causing any special anxiety to their parents. The elder members of the Club and Girls' Committee have been roused to try and grapple with this problem, and they are thankful for the help given by the Fulham Vigilance Committee in the streets and open spaces. If only these young girls can be got within the influence of Clubs, they can be interested in spite of themselves, and made more able to resist the tremendously strong counter-influence of the streets. [5]

Again, in 1925, the optimism was undimmed:

Vigilance work has established itself firmly in Fulham, and Mrs Orton has also organised patrolling during the year in three neighbouring boroughs. Among special events in which we have played our part has been the securing of two Police Women for the Broadway, the closing of a club where young girls were learning to drink, and the improvement of street lighting. [6]

Early in 1926, a meeting at BCH attended by people from an immensely long list of charitable, religious and municipal bodies unanimously passed the following resolution for the attention of the Licensing Magistrates:

This large and representative meeting of persons working in a number of agencies for the uplifting of the people especially amongst the children and young people, wishes to place on record its appreciation of the benefits consequent upon earlier closing as shown by personal observation, namely in the orderly and quiet streets, the gain in health, the quiet Sunday night, and above all the tremendous benefit to children who are saved the long exposure outside the Public House, often in cold and inclement weather, allowing them additional and much needed sleep. We respectfully urge the Bench for the reasons above stated, to adhere to their decision of last year. [7]

On the question of drinking it would seem the campaign had some success; outright temperance was perhaps an impossible target (though there were Trustees who were devoutly for it), but something could be done about drink and young people, even if it required constant returns to the attack. Fifteen years later, the topic remained live, and the Council minutes record a renewed discussion 'regarding the prevalence of the habit of drinking among young people, particularly with reference to the serving of drink to boys and girls of 15-18.' At the same meeting, the Warden reported:

Miss Nye [BCH Youth Leader] took part in a deputation to the Home Secretary, led by the Bishop of Kingston, to appeal for the setting up of a Liquor Control Board. She was given the opportunity, as the only Youth Leader in the deputation, to speak, and afterwards she had a private interview with Sir Herbert Morrison and was able to put her case in more detail. [8]

Back in the twenties however, the 'Vigilance' campaign began to run into difficulties. At an Executive Committee meeting on 14 July 1926, Miss Wickham reported cryptically, and without going into detail, that "It might be necessary to disband the Vigilance Committee." [9] At the next meeting she was again guarded; "The position as regards the Vigilance Committee was still unsettled but it was hoped that Mrs Orton might consent to continue her work. A decision would be come to at a meeting to be held the following week." [10] Three weeks later, she reported to the Council, "Owing to insuperable differences of opinion the Vigilance work as far as BCH is concerned had come to an end." [11] The minutes noted "The Chairman [Mrs Creighton] expressed regret." Mrs Orton, who had evidently been the key worker, left BCH shortly afterwards. The 1926 Annual Report did little to explain the abrupt dénouement:

> Vigilance Work: the disappointments mainly concern several aspects of this work which has had first claim on our resources and hopes for the last four years. It was difficult to describe in former reports what it meant for the Settlement to be the centre of such work with its never ceasing claims on us at all hours of the day or night; and it is still more difficult to explain how or why our hopes miscarried and opportunities for great developments were lost. It is possible, however, to snatch some consolation in three directions.
> (1) A few of our many objects have actually been accomplished and a few dark places lit up.
> (2) Patrolling is still being carried on under other auspices.
> (3) Possibilities are opening out for serving the cause of adolescent girls and boys in other ways. [12]

It remains a matter of speculation what the 'insuperable differences of opinion' were. When the dust had settled Mrs Creighton wrote to Miss Wickham:

20 12 26   Hampton Court Palace

My Dear Miss Wickham
I am afraid that your Christmas at BCH is likely to be rather overshadowed by all the trouble that this upset of the Vigilance work has caused you and Miss Anley. I wish I could have helped you over it, but I can only sympathise, as I know that you feel like everyone else that there is nothing to be done now. Still there remains perhaps the most difficult thing of all, to accept this upset of your plans and hopes without bitterness or any evil feelings, and put it aside and go on in hope. This I am sure you see and are trying to do, and all the thoughts that come to us at this time will be a help. It is really so wonderful the way in which BCH has grown and developed under your fostering care, that perhaps something like a break in its even and prosperous growth may have its lessons to teach. This sounds harsh perhaps, but I don't mean it to. I only feel I should like to take this opportunity of thanking you for all you are doing and of saying how much I feel that beyond all hope and expectation BCH has proved a blessing in Fulham.
Yours Sincerely
Louise Creighton [13]

...

'The cause of adolescent girls and boys' was central to BCH work in the interwar years, and the Settlement ran clubs for both sexes; the mixed 'Guild of Play' for the youngest, Creighton House Club - divided into Juniors and Seniors - for girls, and the Borough Boys' Club, based at Fulham Swimming Baths, with the facilities provided by the borough, and BCH providing the workers. Miss Girdlestone, who ran the boys' club, apparently only missed two club nights in fifteen years. The 1923 Annual Report evoked the worth of the Guild of Play:

> If any justification were needed for our Guild of Play, this last cold winter has more than proved what it means to the children and their parents.
> The more forbidding the weather - fogs, or falling snow, or freezing mud,

so hard on ill-shod feet - the more persistent the successive groups of cold little mortals gathering towards five o'clock at the Club-room door, to be quickly drawn into the brightness and warmth within. Damp shoes and top garments changed, they are soon absorbed in varying pursuits, and when seven o'clock comes, and the evening hymn is sung, it is a warm and happy throng that run away to their homes - too often tragically overcrowded. [14]

A charming cameo emerges from the 1929 Annual Report, talking about the day the Guild of Play was to get first sight of the Christmas Tree:

One little boy, drenched to the skin, presented himself two hours too soon with a tale of mother being at work, the home locked up and himself with nowhere to go. He was too wet and woebegone to be sent away and so got a private view of the preliminary preparations as well as of the tree. [15]

But with the older age groups the work could be demanding, as the 1928 Annual Report made clear:

The task of getting some point of contact with these young creatures grows more and more difficult. As long as they leave school at that most difficult age of 14 and grasp at 'freedom' without understanding its meaning it will continue to be so. The main work of the Club is to stand between them and the wreck of their youth and this has called for all the energy and devotion of the older girls who have fought the fight against the temptations of the factory and workshop and have come through to the knowledge of the great possibilities which clubs open out to their members. [16]

LBHF Archives

**Miss Wickham (L) and some of the senior girls
from Creighton House Club on a picnic sometime in the 1920s.**

One of the most important ways in which BCH stood between children and 'the wreck of their youth' was the work of the Children's Country Holiday Fund. This organisation was founded in 1884 (the same year as Toynbee Hall) to offer holidays in the country, either in camps or in private homes, to deprived children from across the capital. From its start in 1908, BCH threw itself into the workload involved with the

CCHF and, though we do not have figures for every year, it is safe to say that BCH arranged well over 20,000 holidays through the Fund between 1908 and 1995, when the CCHF changed its modus operandi and decided henceforth to work directly through schools rather than local volunteers such as BCH.

BCH

The peak year was 1928 when 928 children were sent away; 781 for a fortnight and 147 'more delicate' children for a month. The workload fell on an Assessment Committee which had to "spend very many hours in the exacting task of deciding on the parents' contributions which range from nothing up to full cost, the average this year [1927] being 12s 4d per fortnight. Where the incomes are quite inadequate we call in the help of the COS to decide whether the holiday should be entirely or nearly free." [17]

This work could obviously sometimes be quite tough and there are regular references throughout the Council and Executive Committee minutes to the way in which many parents would often claim serious financial difficulties in order to get their contribution to the holiday reduced, only then for the child to turn up for the departure in new clothes and carrying very generous pocket money. Almost every year too, there would be a handful of cases of children being returned home early, sometimes because they were just homesick, sometimes because of persistent unacceptable behaviour. Generally though, BCH and the CCHF felt that Fulham's 'return rate' was better than the London-wide average. In at least one case, there was an unexpected and contrary outcome:

> One boy who has visited the same CCHF family in the country for some years, returning under the host family's 'steam' during most school holidays has finally moved in permanently. His family circumstances have been a sad story, but this CCHF family have successfully applied, with consent on all sides, to foster this little boy. [18]

The health benefits of a CCHF holiday are self-evident, but there could also be an educational dividend, as the 1931 Annual Report revealed:

> Children from eleven schools were sent away for country holidays of two or more weeks. Among many delightful episodes remaining in the minds of those whose gladly given work made this possible is that of a small boy, who came flying round to ask with shining eyes, whether it was true, where he was going, "plums grew on *trees*" - the BCH visitor having told his mother that he was going to a village in a plum-growing district. [19]

Finally, another recurrent theme across BCH history; if a particular individual had an idea or felt there was a field of useful action where she could contribute, she could just get on with it. The work might last only as long as she was around, and cease with her moving on, but an impression had been made, on the life of the Settlement, but more especially on the young beneficiaries. The 1927 Annual Report has a classic:

> Mention must be made of the little unofficial needlework class taken on Thursday evenings by Dorothy Harley, the Club member who spent 1926 as a student at the Working Women's College. To this class come those rather shy, undersized and backward juniors of 14 to 15 years of age, who feel looked down upon by the usually very 'grown-up' young persons of this same age. Dorothy Harley's quiet influence must make a difference to these real child wage-earners when they are working, as they must, among not always very desirable influences. [20]

***

THE PREMISES

"Some of the healing 'miracles' lay in the changed attitude
of a mother to an unwanted or difficult child."

Miss Wickham [1]

BCH expanded its premises twice in the interwar years and both times the physical expansion was mirrored by an extension to the range of the Settlement's activities. First mention of the possibility of acquiring No 380 Lillie Road, and thus occupying the whole of the original Emily Terrace, came at an Executive Committee meeting in July 1918, but it was not until November 1924 that BCH finally obtained 'vacant possession', after a six-year saga of wrangles with a constitutionally intransigent sitting tenant. The story is funny in retrospect, but must have been galling at the time because plans were laid, with LCC support, to start a Children's Clinic at No 380 in 1921, and these plans could not be realised until 1925.

When the Clinic finally opened, on 1 April 1925, it was with detailed financial support from the LCC: £200 for initial equipment, £66 per annum for the Doctor at the Minor Ailments Clinic (1 session a week), £300 per annum for the Dentist (5 sessions a week), £37-10 per annum for the Anaesthetist (1 session a fortnight), £20 per annum maintenance, £25 per annum rent contribution; plus capitation, 660 cases per annum in the Minor Ailments Clinic at 1/- each, and 1540 cases per annum in the Dental Clinic at 2/- each; plus, for occasional use of the premises for School Medical Inspections, £10 per annum. It rapidly became clear that the demands for the services would far exceed initial predictions; in the first two months, the Dental Clinic dealt with 341 cases, and the Minor Ailments Clinic averaged 400 callers a week. The 1925 Annual Report noted, "Special events have ranged from an inspection of the clinic by a League of Nations' party of continental doctors to arrivals, in the mood of paying a ceremonial call, of parents who, despite appeals, blandishments, and even the NSPCC, had refused for years to have their children 'tampered with.'" [2]

By February 1926, the LCC had sanctioned extra sessions each week in both Minor Ailments and the Dental Clinic, and agreed to the Anaesthetist being weekly rather than fortnightly. By the end of 1926 Minor Ailments were up to 750 callers a week, and by July 1927 the flow was reportedly 'overwhelming' with sometimes 200 callers a day. The Annual Report evoked the atmosphere:

> The congestion in our small rooms has been sometimes very great.
> Miss Russell[3] has a faithful band of helpers who mitigate this, and make
> the waiting times fruitful by story-telling and friendship-making. Thanks
> to them and to the kindness of the nurses the children who crowd in with
> sores and other 'minor ailments' - often the result of overcrowding and

insanitary home conditions - go away with increased happiness as well as with white bandages or cleansing lotions. [4]

A bizarre passing insight into medical practice eighty years ago comes from an Executive Committee meeting of December 1928, where it was reported, "As a result of complaints from the nurses about the washing of bandages, they were trying cheaper bandages which could be thrown away after use." [5] It was later minuted that overall the throwaway bandages had proved slightly more expensive, but more satisfactory on the hygiene front.

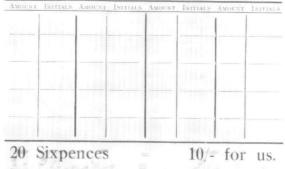

BCH

A typical BCH Appeal card of the 1930s.
Left with local households, it was hoped to raise
small but regular contributions.

Children's medical services at BCH proved so popular, not only with local people but with the Town Hall as well, that other departments were added; an Ionization clinic in 1930, Vision in 1931, Hearing in 1932, Child Guidance in 1933 and Nutrition in 1937. Also based at BCH, after the Infant Welfare Centre in Greyhound Road (originally the 'School for Mothers') closed, was Miss Christian Wickham's massage clinic, which garnered lavish praise:

24th October 1929

Dear Miss Wickham
Doubtless you will wonder who is writing you, but I felt I must just thank you so much for all you have done for our darling grandson Derek Fillingham. I cannot express how indebted we are to you for all you have done for him and I am sure you must be very happy to know how you are curing the dear children and comforting the poor mothers. So please accept our heartfelt thanks.

Yours very sincerely
Grandma and Grandpa French [6]

BCH [7]

The Massage Clinic was described as 'a veritable Pool of Bethesda,' and the 1934 Annual Report enthused, "Over 80 babies were treated by Miss Christian Wickham during 1934 and many hundreds since she first started the clinic in 1920. It is wonderful to think of the straightened limbs and quieted nerves and readjustment, physical and mental, that have been the result of her massage and influence." [8]

The most innovative of the clinics were Child Guidance and Nutrition. The Child Guidance Clinic, which opened 22 November 1933, was the first in the country to function as an integral part of a Settlement. Writing in the 1936 Annual Report, the Hon Medical Director, Sydney Mitchell reported:

> Typical cases include lack of self-confidence, temper tantrums, bed wetting, educational difficulties, stealing and general home maladjustments resulting in childhood unhappiness. By a team approach to the child individually, its parents and any others in close contact with it, we seek to help each child through its incoherent fears and longings to a happy security. Two cases may be quoted as typical of the work we do: An only child of 10 was referred for pains in the stomach associated with arithmetic lessons! He was found to be of good average intelligence, but his reading and spelling were at a 7½ year old level and he failed to score any marks in the tests for fundamental processes in mathematics. He had missed a lot of time from school owing to illness. Coaching was arranged and after five months he had risen from third from the bottom of his class of 43 to top of a class of 43. Whereas previously he had only got 1 out of 50 for reading, his last marks were 45 out of 50. He also looks forward to arithmetic lessons with pleasure and the pains have disappeared. In the second case: A boy of 2½ was referred for jealousy of the baby of 4 months, sleeplessness and refusal to eat. The father had lost patience and beaten him. The child was of good average intelligence and expressed in play with plasticene and toys, fears of both parents. He has been encouraged to play out his difficulties. After two months he now sleeps and feeds well, is friendly with his parents and is very nice to the baby ... Although we have so far confined our work to cases from the Boroughs of Fulham, Hammersmith and Chelsea, we have already been obliged to establish a waiting list. [9]

In the next Annual Report, after outlining an ever-expanding caseload, the Clinic's Director concluded, "In view of our long waiting list, there is an undoubted need for a Clinic of this nature in the neighbourhood. The future of the Clinic is a matter of some anxiety; it may be impossible to continue indefinitely on a voluntary basis." [10]

If we follow the story of the Child Guidance Clinic through to its closure, we can see a shift of emphasis which is a microcosm of changes across the whole of BCH. The Child Guidance Sub-Committee was chaired by Mrs Warren Pearl, a woman whose generosity regularly helped the Clinic over various financial hurdles. At a meeting on 3 December 1942 for example, "The Hon Treasurer said we really had not the funds to meet the new payments to the secretary and for the typist. The Chairman most generously increased her subscription to £50." [11] But a year later the Director was beginning to chafe:

> There was really no future for voluntary clinics unless teaching could be part of its work. The general tendency among local authorities was to pay fees. They could not expect to find experienced people to work for them on a voluntary basis. The LCC must be made to feel its responsibilities. Many thanks were due to our Chairman and other benefactors for their generosity, but the LCC must face the fact whether they wanted Child Guidance Clinics. [12]

As the war drew on, the Director was reporting yet further growth in the caseload, and a proliferation, hardly surprising, in war-related difficulties among the children referred to the Clinic, which only briefly closed during the Flying Bomb period in 1944:

In the figures already reported probation cases were an increasing factor. A new peak period of delinquency was being reached and there would be another peak period when the final return home came. The pattern of life was broken, no strong moral sense had been built up, the pattern was disrupted, there would be no restraint ... [The Director] said we could see the form of case coming up out of evacuation, the form of ego continuity, a conversation of I's. They were aggressively superior, most unhappy, everything they did put them out of contact with other children. They have no weak points. Another type of child was the one who had had no experience of discipline. [13]

Finally, with the war won, Mrs Warren Pearl faced the facts, "The Chairman herself had more than half supported the Clinic in the past but she felt that this was no longer business-like and that other arrangements should be made. [She thought] the LCC should be invited to take over entirely." [14] In fact the Child Guidance Clinic soldiered on at Lillie Road until 1950, but then indeed the LCC took over and moved the operation to 25 Stratford Road W8.

...

The second particularly innovative medical service begun at BCH in the 1930s was the Nutrition Clinic, which arose when the International Federation of University Women referred a refugee German, Dr Lili Meyer-Wedell, to the Settlement in 1936. Child nutrition was then a new field in medicine and she had done pioneering work in Germany. She rapidly impressed the medical staff at BCH, and at her suggestion BCH convened a lunch on 26 February 1937, attended by representatives of the Ministry of Health and the LCC, along with Fulham's Medical Officer of Health, and the upshot was she was given the go-ahead to open for business on 11 June. Her methods were outlined in the 1937 Annual Report:

> Each child is given a complete overhaul: blood test, examination of cardiac condition, height and weight, muscular tension, dynamometer reading etc. Von Pirquet's Pelidisi Index [correlating a child's *sitting* height to its weight] is used for ascertaining the English norm as compared with international standards. A report on food given in the home for a week is obtained in order to gain some idea of the average daily diet of each case. Whenever needed and possible, a special diet is prepared for each child, and the mid-day meal is taken in our Invalid Kitchen, 'supper' sandwiches being taken home. [15]

Dr Meyer-Wedell's work was so convincing that the LCC proposed to take over after only eighteen months, but unfortunately they decided to dispense with her services, on account of recurrent problems with her poor English. The Council, on 6 October 1938, had to decide whether to accept:

> Miss Dickson read a report from Dr Meyer-Wedell on her work and aims, and said that she thought Dr Meyer-Wedell was very clever and was doing most excellent work, but that there was the difficulty of language as she spoke English very badly. Miss Wickham suggested that it would be a great pity if Dr Meyer-Wedell's work was given up altogether, and that a place should be found for her in the new scheme. Other members felt that the Settlement ought not to risk losing the LCC offer ... the Council was divided. [16]

Sadly, the imperative of going along with the paymasters prevailed, and while the clinic continued, Dr Meyer-Wedell disappeared from BCH's records.

...

Whatever the medical dividends of the various clinics, together they had a tangible educative effect in the interwar years. The 1938 Annual Report:

Twenty years ago it was uphill work to persuade parents to consent to have a child's tooth stopped (we were often told that 'Father suffered agony through having his teeth stopped when in the Army; neither of us hold with it anyway') - now the majority readily give their consent to any necessary treatment, and workers very often tell me how much they wish there had been school clinics when they went to school, and many we knew as schoolgirls are now bringing their own children, which speaks for itself. [17]

On the other hand, from the child's point of view, going to the dentist never was a favourite outing, and a Mrs Kenworthy, writing to BCH in 1990 when she was '72 years young', recalled, "Beforehand a lady used to come in showing us kids a snow scene in a glass case to take our minds of the coming ordeal." [18] 82-year-old Jim Smith today recalls the dentist without illusions, "We all thought he was a bit of a butcher, we were all scared of him, he looked so awesome and he wore a rubber apron." [19] And Joyce Warmington had similarly bleak memories, "It was a horrific experience, and there was a horrid boy who said they would keep me here forever if the bleeding didn't stop." [20]

All the clinics discussed so far were aimed at the children of the locality, but there was one other which should get a mention - designed for the mothers bringing their children in, it offered chiropody; 1/- one foot or 1/6 for two, charges set so low "that many poor women suffering agonies with their feet can be relieved at a cost which suits their circumstances." [21] It opened on 6 April 1938, with £20 donated by a well-wisher for the equipment, and £50 per annum promised from Fulham Borough Council to pay the chiropodist. In its first year it saw 204 patients and gave 427 treatments; "The relief expressed by the women after their visit is a most heartening thing to witness." [22] One other benefit for mothers, that evidently came as a surprise to some of them, was the Women's Holiday Fund, the Fulham branch run by BCH, a charity set up to give poor women a break from the domestic grind. There are several affecting letters of gratitude in BCH archives, of which the following give a flavour:

One mother who had been coping with delicate children and every kind of difficulty with no respite for many years, wrote from Shanklin on her holiday "I must have been born under a lucky star." [23]
The weather is grand and the flowers simply lovely. The matron is very sweet and she makes us very much at home. Mrs D, the other lady from Fulham, is also enjoying herself. I don't think either of us has walked and laughed so much in our lives, but all good things must come to an end, so I will close.
Now remaining, Yours most gratefully, Rose B. [24]

...

As with the acquisition of 380 Lillie Road, there was a gap between the first reference to the Garden House (as it would become known) and its eventual purchase; at an Executive Committee meeting on 14 November 1928, mention was made of the Midget Lamp factory, housed in a brick block to the rear of BCH, which was closing down, and, it was suggested, would be a very useful addition to BCH premises, offering space for club activities, and suggesting possibilities for Adult Education classes. A slip sheet was hurriedly prepared and inserted into the 1929 Annual Report with the heading A GREAT OPPORTUNITY, and going on to say, in part:

Some factory premises adjoining our garden have fallen vacant and seem quite obviously to ask to be incorporated in the Settlement. They would need much adapting and beautifying, but it is estimated that the comparatively small sum of £2000 would buy the freehold and pay for all the necessary work. [25]

Skipping the tedious hold-ups and setbacks (such as the discovery of dry rot in the floorboards), the Garden House was ready for a royal opening on 25 February 1931:

BCH

The Garden House opening: L-R, Miss Wickham, HRH Princess Helena Victoria, Prebendary P. S. G. Propert, Colonel Waldron, the Mayor of Fulham, and Mrs Sarah Bailey, Vice-Chairman of BCH Trustees.

The Annual Report for 1930-31 listed a host of inaugural events:

Occasions in the nature of 'house warming' were two performances by the club of the striking Christmas Play *Every Man in Every Street* and a series of Sunday evening concerts with larger audiences than the old club room, charming as it is for chamber music, could have contained. The other rooms, away from the noisy street, are a great boon for meetings and office work, and we are glad of more space for storing paraphernalia - from dramatic properties to case papers ... Apart from its symbolic and adventuring aspects the Garden House brings relief to the old premises which have been too fully used during the past year ... It has become a playground for Miss Russell's swarms of children. Hardly is the Guild of Play dismissed when the Club takes possession with classes and recreation

64

of all kinds. On Sundays the Mission Sunday School has filled it and all other available rooms, while in the evening after Church hours a rapt audience has listened to beautiful music. [26]

BCH

Summer 1933: breakfast for the residents in the garden.
Miss Wickham presides at the right end of the table.
The Garden House behind, showing the long single window
of the main hall on the first floor.
Picture taken by Dr Heinsheimer, one of several German refugees
given succour by BCH in the 1930s.

The Garden House continued to serve a variety of functions right up to and through the 1950s, including Olde Tyme Dancing ("Who would ever forget Miss Florence's cheerful 'Now come along darlings!' as she encourages even the most heavy-footed of us to prance round the room!" [27]), housing an Invalid Kitchen, being let for wedding receptions, and hosting large meetings of a range of affiliated organizations like Toc H. But in 1959, the Treasurer put it to the Trustees that the Garden House could raise valuable funds for BCH if it was to be commercially let out, and duly Messrs Floral Reproductions became tenants. Subsequently, in 1965, in an arrangement with the British Council, the Garden House was converted into four flats as accommodation for overseas students, which lasted until the 1990s. Since then it has continued to be rented, through the St Mungo Community Trust.

There is a curious footnote to the Garden House story: in September 1960, BCH had a letter from the De Havilland Aircraft Company seeking permission to put a plaque on the Garden House, it having been the workshop where Sir Geoffrey de Havilland built his first two planes in 1909 and 1910. The Trustees were only too happy to go along with the proposal but, sadly, after one further letter, nothing more was heard. But the story is true, and confirmed in Sir Geoffrey's autobiography *Sky Fever*:

I found a shed in Bothwell Street, Fulham which seemed to meet our needs, and it was only one pound per week ... In November 1909 most of the work in the Fulham workshop was finished. The premises were not large enough to take our [No 1] aeroplane fully erected, so we hired a lorry and drove it down in bits [to Seven Barrows, Hampshire], together with the engine and tools. [28]

***

"NOT IN ALL RESPECTS
REASONABLY FIT
FOR HUMAN HABITATION"

"It's hard to know how to be decent." [1]

The history of relations between BCH and the local authorities has largely been a tale without disharmony, both sides seeking to maximise the alliance to mutual satisfaction. But on one topic there was a time when BCH placed itself in the van of a campaign that was by no means welcome among all who sat in the council chamber.

It will be recalled from Chapter Four that Fulham, with its rapid growth in the last decades of the nineteenth century, had been dubiously blessed by all the arts and skills of the jerry builder. Whole swathes of the housing then thrown up were more or less instantly dilapidated, and by the 1920s had declined even further. The Borough's population in 1921 was 157,938, giving a ratio of .96 rooms per head, but five years later the population had risen to 164,300 while little or no addition was made to the housing stock. BCH's Annual Report for 1926, mentioning the subject for the first time, fired a warning shot:

> Fulham is one of the boroughs where the percentage of serious overcrowding is high and the tragic results of such conditions meet us at every turn. A few social workers, feeling that the time was ripe for some concerted efforts in the matter, have been meeting lately at the Settlement and hope, with the valuable help of Miss Lupton, to formulate some proposals soon. [2]

Miss Anne Lupton had arrived at BCH in 1926. She must have had qualities that caught Miss Wickham's eye because when it was decided that housing should be taken up as a cause, Miss Lupton was asked to handle the campaign. Writing her obituary in 1967, Miss Wickham recalled her response, "I know nothing about housing but I will have a try at it." [3] The upshot, within a year, was the formation of the Fulham Housing Association to agitate and the Fulham Housing Improvement Society to put ideas into action, both with Miss Lupton as Hon Secretary. And the first product of this swirl of activity was a specially-commissioned report on housing in the borough by two women members of the Surveyors' Institute. Miss Barclay and Miss Perry pulled no punches, quoting early on from the *Fulham Chronicle* of 11 March 1927, reporting an inquest into a baby who had suffocated while sleeping with its parents:

> The Deputy Coroner said "He sympathised with the parents in the conditions under which they lived, but at the same time he hoped the case would be a warning, inasmuch as it was distinctly dangerous for mothers to take young children in bed with them." [4]

They went on to produce a catalogue of particulars that evoke the horrors of the *Bitter Cry* [see p 5 above]. They found, for example, at a house in Hannell Road:

2 semi-basement rooms

Living in the *Front Room* is a man, his wife, and three children. The tenant states he has to do his own repairs, but the agent provides the materials - taking months to do so.

Living in the *Back Room* (8' x 9') is a man, his wife, and two children. This room is in a horrible condition - the tenant complains of rats, mice, beetles and spiders, and bugs. The floor is in a bad state, and the hearth is full of holes. During the flood [June 1927] the house was flooded so badly that there was over 3ft. of water, sewage, etc. in the Basement. Oilcloth had to be taken up and burned; clothes, etc. were spoilt. In spite of the damp the bugs are very bad, and the tenants are kept awake at night with them. There is a small wash-house attached in the yard. The W.C. is infested by rats, and we are told that even the frying-pans hanging up in the wash-house had feet marks of rats on them. [5]

Overall, they typically encountered:

Serious structural and sanitary defects: unpointed brickwork, sagging window arches and crumbling door jambs, sunken piers, leaning chimney stacks, leaking roofs, missing and broken gutters and rain-water pipes. In many more cases, houses (usually built from 50 to 70 years ago) are sound and outwardly in fair condition, but a survey of the interior reveals a general state of verminous plaster and woodwork, dirty and crumbling walls and ceilings, defective flooring and window sashes, and broken grates, coppers, and locks. The complete absence of locks is a common feature. [6]

LBHF Archives

The rear of Nos 20-28 Heckfield Place.

Towards the end they cited, by way of support, the 1926 Fulham Medical Officer of Health's Report:

> 3072 houses were inspected for housing defects, and 13,690 re-inspections were made. (of these 3072 houses, 1593 were found 'not in all respects reasonably fit for human habitation'). Of the 3072 inspections, 2130 were in consequence of complaint, either by tenants or by Health Visitors, Tuberculosis Nurses, etc., 719 in consequence of infectious disease, and only 223 were house-to-house inspections. [7]

The Mayor of Fulham, Colonel Sir William Waldron, given a private sight of the Report ahead of publication, is remembered as saying, "If this is made public it will force the hands of the Council and landlords will be ruined." [8] He and the entire Borough Council were summoned by the Bishop of London, Arthur Winnington-Ingram, BCH's abiding friend ever since he had opened the Settlement in 1908, to attend at Fulham Palace for a formal presentation of the Report's findings. Astonishingly, there were some councillors who felt the matter was not a municipal concern, and took refuge behind the mantra of not adding a penny to the rates. These were still the days when 'state' interference, even at a municipal level, was regarded with suspicion in some quarters.

The BCH campaigners were determined that the Town Hall should be made to take its responsibilities on housing seriously and in the run-up to the 1928 municipal elections, the FHA mounted a publicity campaign that could not easily be ignored. Flyers headed **BOROUGH COUNCIL ELECTIONS AND THE HOUSING PROBLEM** were distributed through letter boxes to the entire electorate. After giving a short summary of the Barclay & Perry Report, they went on:

> **Who is Responsible**
> Large powers have been conferred on Borough Councils by Parliament both for building and for remedying insanitary conditions. **It is therefore of the utmost importance** that on the 1ˢᵗ November a Council shall be elected in Fulham which will be prepared to make use of these powers to the fullest extent, so that this blot on the Borough may be removed.
> **Each Elector therefore is Responsible**
> No Borough Council can act without the support of public opinion.
> **Each Citizen therefore is Responsible**
> It may be necessary to spend money, but we must be prepared to make sacrifices in order that this scandal to a Christian community may be removed from our midst.
> >   (signed)   AF London
> >   (President, Fulham Housing Association.)
> >   P. S. G. Propert
> >   (Chairman, Fulham Housing Association.) [9]

At the same time every candidate, whatever their political complexion, received a letter from Miss Lupton:

> Dear Sir (or Madam)
> My Committee, having heard that you are a Candidate for election to the Fulham Borough Council, directs me to ask you to be good enough to reply to the following question
> > "Will you support a policy for the provision of new houses or self-contained and suitable tenements, especially for the lower

paid members of the working classes, within or accessible from
the Borough: and for the acquisition, adaptation and improvement
of existing houses, even if this policy involves an increase in the
rates?"
I shall be glad to receive your reply as soon as possible.
Yours Faithfully
AM Lupton
Hon Secretary (Fulham Housing Association) [10]

It should not be thought that the Council was impervious to the campaign; for most of
the 1920's Fulham was dominated by the Municipal Reformers Party, formerly known
as the Moderates, and known to the *Fulham Chronicle* as Conservatives. Although
Labour had beaten them in the immediate aftermath of World War I, they were to
hold power in the borough until Labour's decisive return to power in 1934. The MR
were not natural bedfellows with the housing campaigners, and they were of course, in
the way of Conservatives always, determined not to inflate the rates. And their hands
had been to some extent tied earlier in the 1920s by the limitation of their powers; they
could inspect, and occasionally issue closing orders, but the mechanisms for moving
against negligent landlords were laborious. By the time of Miss Lupton's campaign, the
Metropolitan Borough of Fulham had only so far managed to erect 401 council flats at
Wyfold House, compared with nearly twice that number put up by private philanthropy
such as the Peabody and Samuel Lewis Trusts.

The pressure put on the Council, by the Fulham Housing Association, by BCH, and by
public opinion, was such that Miss Wickham could Report to a BCH Council meeting
on 31 January 1929 that "the attitude of the Borough Council had changed and that
they were considering a building scheme." And again, at an Executive Committee
meeting three months later, she announced, "(a) that the Borough Council has decided
to apply for compulsory powers to obtain a building site, and (b) that it was thought
that a large deputation of Fulham social workers had had some effect." [11]

This project, though the pressure had to be maintained, was the purchase of the Swan
Brewery site, between the Fulham Road and Eelbrook Common, on which the Council
eventually erected Fulham Court in 1934. But, for example, the notorious 'Avenues' on
the other side of Fulham Road - Lodge Avenue, Rock Avenue, Walham Avenue and
Lurgan Avenue - which were cited by Barclay & Perry as prime examples of slums, and
which had been picked out as long ago as 1899 by Charles Booth, "occupied by rough
Irish labourers and costers and the lowest class of prostitute", were not demolished
until after World War II and today's Lancaster Court built in their place. It is no
wonder that 23,000 people are said to have left Fulham between the wars in search of
better living conditions.

While the Fulham Housing Association agitated, the Fulham Housing Improvement
Society was dealing practically with bricks and mortar. The 1928 BCH Annual Report
appealed:
> The FHIS, whose Management Committee has met every week at the
> Settlement, has raised during the year nearly £8000 in shares, loan stock
> and gifts, but the work now in hand - building flats and reconditioning
> slum dwellings - will cost another £7000, while there is an unlimited field

for further enterprise. Nothing to which BCH has set its hand during its 21 years, just completed, has been of more importance than these efforts to help its neighbours suffering from bad housing and overcrowding, and we hope our associates will make widely known both the need for money and the sound basis of the FHIS. [12]

The 1929 Annual Report was proud to report:

> The real reward to the pioneers who took shares and loan stock or gave donations has lain in the actual accomplishment of more than we dared dream of when we fired the beacon nearly three years ago. Thirteen new flats have been opened which have given new life to the hard pressed families who have moved into them, while 're-conditioning' has made great improvements in houses formerly in terrible disrepair with only one water tap to serve three families. [13]

In 1930 the FHA and FHIS, though still a proud entry in the BCH Annual Reports, moved their headquarters to 91 Dawes Road. The properties they had built or re-conditioned were managed along 'Octavia Hill' lines, that is the tenants were encouraged towards thrift, towards being house-proud and towards a communal consciousness of the overall state of the building they shared. The rent collectors sought a more personal relationship, bordering on friendship, with the tenants they managed, whilst maintaining, as Octavia Hill always insisted they should, an unbending sternness to any falling behind in rent payments. They hoped that the Borough Council would also run its rented properties along these lines, but the Depression put paid to that. The 1931 Annual Report lamented:

> High hopes that the Borough Council's building of new flats might achieve a solution of the housing problem in Fulham have met with much disappointment. Slum clearance and other schemes which ought to have gone on simultaneously - being only possible while there is available space for re-housing - have melted away under the stress of the national difficulties. [14]

Of the properties new-built by the FHIS in their 1930s heyday, most are no longer around, largely thanks to the Luftwaffe. But one development does survive:

BCH

'Brightwells', opened by HRH Princess Alice, 16 July 1936.

71

I quote from the Fulham History Society's *History of Fulham*:

The 'Brightwells' scheme was the idea of Mr JH Palmer JP, to build on a piece of land that was left by the late Miss Charlotte Sulivan in the care of the London Gardens Association for the purpose of a playground for children. The ground was used to build flats to house families from Campbell Street, which was then turned into a playground instead ... 'Brightwells' cost over £17,000 and was built without cost to the ratepayers, on capital subscribed by old friends of the FHIS. Built of mellow red brick, it contains thirty flats, six with roof gardens, and consists of a three-storied central block flanked by flat roofed wings around an open space maintained as a garden common to all the tenants ... The architect was Miss J. F. Abram LRIBA. Opening 'Brightwells,' Princess Alice said that she "felt sure that the flats offered accommodation and modern devices for reducing the arduous labours of the housewife." [15]

Whatever the impact of the Barclay & Perry Report, the problems of housing in Fulham proved stubbornly intractable. Ten years on, in the 1937 Annual Report, Miss Baber, the second Warden, made clear her despair:

Please do not think 'the slums have been cleared away.' Here in Fulham, the Borough Council is making strenuous efforts to cope with the housing situation, and so in a smaller way, is our own Fulham Housing Improvement Society. But patches remain which are as bad as any existing in the dark days which most people believe to be in the dim and distant past. We made a survey of a certain street in the Borough, in which cases of overcrowding were very numerous, in the families of which there was a terrible record of sickness and malnutrition ... Sometimes I ask myself how we can all live among it, meeting these conditions day by day, doing ambulance work indeed, but so little in the way of passionate protest against this degradation of personalities. "Oh why and for what are we waiting, while our brothers droop and die, and on every wind of heaven, a wasted life goes by?" [16]

The FHIS built nothing new after 'Brightwells', the war and post-war austerity saw to that, but it had one further and still extant contribution to make. In 1952, with support from the LCC and Fulham Old People's Welfare Committee, after a search lasting four years for suitable premises, it purchased Putney Hill House to be Fulham's first old people's home. Fulham had the highest percentage of old-age pensioners in the Metropolitan area, the need was self-evident, and, strange as it may now seem, the Borough then had no powers to start old people's homes. Refurbished and renamed Royston, it was opened in January 1953 to its first thirty residents. Ten years later, part of the large garden at Royston was sacrificed to the building of Wickham House, offering twenty-four new flats. Then, at a Council Meeting in 1965, came a short and simple *coup de grace*:

FHIS: Miss GP Willson is retiring at the end of this month. This has forced the Society to re-assess costs of administration and after much thought and discussion it seems most likely that the Society will amalgamate with the Rowe Housing Trust. [17]

The amalgamation took place eventually on 1 January 1968, shortly after Miss Anne Lupton MBE, the indefatigable spearhead of both the FHA and the FHIS in their pre-war days, died, after a long and painful illness bravely borne.

***

EMERGENCY

> "As I write the sirens are sounding; are we going to let the forces
> of evil prevent us from serving our neighbours? Surely not."
> Last sentence of BCH Letter to America, 1940 [1]

Whereas the outbreak of World War One had come as something of a shock to the British in 1914, World War Two had plainly been in the offing since the early 1930s. If nothing else sounded alarm bells, from 1933 onwards, BCH had given shelter to a succession of German refugees who had 'lost her job on racial grounds' or had 'a nasty encounter with the Gestapo.' Municipal war planning was discussed at a BCH Council meeting as early as 1938:

> A letter was read from the Fulham Air Raid Precautions Department
> enquiring into the possibility of making an Air Raid Shelter at the Settlement. The
> Council agreed as a matter of policy that it would be their aim that in a national
> emergency the Settlement should be of the fullest service to the neighbourhood. [2]

It was decided that BCH premises were not suitable for a public Air Raid Shelter, but should be offered as a First Aid Post, acting as a satellite to the main Emergency Receiving Station at Cobbs Hall in the Fulham Palace Road. Also in 1938, BCH workers helped out with the fitting and explanation of gas masks for children in several local schools. But, for all the advance warnings, there was still a very British period of confusion when the war did finally officially break out. Some BCH residents were called immediately away into various wartime jobs, so the redoubtable Miss Wickham, now 65, came back in to help in a range of ways. One of the earliest responses to the war was the setting up of Citizens' Advice Bureaux, one at the Charity Organisation Society office in Kempson Road, and one at BCH. In the first month, the BCH CAB had 223 enquiries, in the second month 116, and in the third to sixth months 208. By January 1940 the 'phony war' had abated the initial anxieties and the Council was told, "CAB work has almost faded away. People seem largely to have adjusted themselves to wartime living now. We have only had 45 applications this month." [3]

In this early period of brittle calm, BCH was more than ever welcome as a refuge:

> At the moment, the Settlement appears to be the only place in Fulham,
> except the public houses, which is open at night, and which offers a
> cheerful normal atmosphere to young people, who are thankful to have
> somewhere to turn in from the dark streets. "It's a real blessing this Club
> and no mistake, I think it's a grand idea," said a boy the other night. "The
> best afternoon we've had since the war started," said a woman at their
> opening social. [4]

Another service BCH performed at the beginning of the war, just as it had done in 1914, was opening a Sunday club for German and Austrian refugees in the area "as a gesture of friendship to many who were at that time threatened with unjust treatment" [5], at least until they were all interned in the summer of 1940. Then, with Dunkirk and the fall of France, it became clear the war really was on. Miss Baber reported to the Council:

> Since last Council meeting, our work has changed in character. The Clubs for boys, girls and women have practically collapsed. The boys and girls started coming at nights, but the sirens went almost as soon as they arrived and they have had to disperse.
>
> Our main work has lain in two directions:- a) help with the Emergency Feeding Centres, b) greatly increased CAB work owing to rush of mothers and babies and old people to evacuate. Emergency Feeding Centres; these come under the Public Assistance Authorities - but when the first rush of homeless, due to time bombs or destruction of houses, started, everything was in a hopeless state of confusion. We have laboured to get conditions better by stirring up our LCC members and by sleeping nights in the schools to help with the babies, the old and the sick. [6]

On the night of 8 October 1940, at 9.30pm, the war came directly to BCH itself, in the form of a High Explosive bomb. A correspondent to BCH's 'Living Memories Group' offered a picture of the night:

> My parents lived in the basement flat of St Clement's Mansions next to Bishop Creighton House … When the air raids were getting bad my mother went to live with relations in Gloucestershire … My father was the only resident in the block to go to the air raid shelters in the recreation ground opposite every night. One night the block received a direct hit and all were killed [LBHF Archive records show three residents were killed that night, and another eight people, including children, were killed in the shelter across the road]. A Mr Hughes, resident on the first floor, died in hospital, he lived long enough to recall that he was shaving at the time, heard a 'crunch' and just caught a glimpse of the fins of a bomb disappearing through the floor to explode in my father's flat below … I can recall viewing the demolished premises the next day and seeing the street sign 'BOTHWELL ST' laying in the rubble. Thankfully my parents were both well and lived to a good old age. [7]

A week later, Miss Baber reported to Council:

> The residents were all in their small shelter [that is, the reinforced basement of No 380], except one. The Clinic House was demolished and the neighbouring block of flats fell at the same time. The residents were entombed by the falling masonry - but Miss Gore, who was outside the shelter [she'd gone to make tea], got the police and within a very few minutes an exit was cut through and the residents were able to get out before the gas fumes had had time to become too powerful. They spent the night in the public trenches until the morning when they were able to return to the Garden House. The LCC Surveyor came to see the houses and went over the property with the Warden and Miss Wickham.
> a) The Garden House is undamaged except for a few panes of glass and work can be carried on from these premises.
> b) The Clinic House is entirely demolished. Some of the equipment has been salvaged, including the dental chair in a damaged condition. Two bedrooms were carried away in this house and all contents lost … The boxroom has not yet been excavated. Some salvage may be made.
> c) The next house [No 378] - containing the dining room, Warden's sitting room, CAB office and two bedrooms - is so badly damaged as to be unusable.

This will be boarded up by the Police, and no rates will be payable in respect of it. Practically all the furniture was saved and has been stored in the next house. d) The next house and the next again [Nos 376 and 374] - containing the large club room, the chapel, the basement rooms, the common room and six bedrooms - are practically undamaged except for broken windows, and all the contents are safe. On the whole, we have lost amazingly little furniture, and the two houses can speedily be put into order for use, with the exception of the office which must be used as a furniture store for the present. The heating arrangements and kitchen premises were in the damaged and unsafe house. e) The Garden Hut was completely destroyed [The Garden Hut was a modest wooden edifice with a verandah, erected in 1936 in memory of Mrs Creighton. It would not be rebuilt]. [8]

LBHF Archives

9 October 1940.

Giving no reason (not that was minuted), Miss Baber proposed to the Council at the same meeting that Miss Gore, saviour on the night of the bomb, should be given one month's notice. Why? History is not to know. Council agreed, but softened the blow by formally thanking Miss Gore for her prompt action in getting the police and by clubbing together 21/- to buy her 'a nice handbag'. The staff also subscribed money for the presentation of two silver cigarette cases to the policemen who effected the rescue.

Reshuffling, one or two clinics moved temporarily to other premises, the rest moved elsewhere in BCH. The work carried on with barely a hiccup. These were the days when Britain was anxious to get the USA into the war on our side, and Jim Smith - he who had not liked visiting the dentist at BCH in the 1930s - recalls a radio programme in which he and other youngsters, broadcasting from BCH, answered questions from American teenagers about the blitz, rationing and life in wartime. BCH also sent regular letters to supporters in America, and in one of late 1940, they told their US friends a story that could stand alone as a justification for the existence of Settlements independent of municipal or government bureaucracies:

A man, accompanied by his brother-in-law, arrived in a state of collapse.
He had run out of his house when a bomb fell upon it; his wife had run into
one shelter and he into another. The shelter in which his wife had taken refuge
had received a direct hit. It was several days before he discovered her body in
the mortuary. She had had with her in her handbag all her valuables, including
her insurance policy, marriage lines etc. What could he do? He was quite
incapable of doing anything for himself. The last straw had been when some
ignorant official had asked him, "What do you value your wife at - £20?"
The Settlement worker arranged for an immediate grant for clothes from the
Assistance Board, got the death certificate from the Town Hall, arranged with the
Insurance Society about the burial. The man was given a hot bath and a cup of
tea, and sent away a little less dazed, a little more collected, knowing what to do,
and grateful beyond words for the help received. [9]

Support arrived in many forms and from many places; there was, for example, all through the war, an annual gift of money towards a Christmas party at BCH, sent by the school children of Northern Rhodesia (today's Zambia). Those parties are a fond memory for Helen Macdonald:

"I was a blitzkid and as my father was very ill there was not much joy in our
household, what with the bombing raids and rationing. It must have been
around Christmas that we were invited to a party at BCH. We came into the hall
and had tea, probably arranged by Sheila Parish or her relatives, and we had
games and then we were each given a present. When I got home I found I had a
box of sweets (a whole box, unheard of!). These sweets were sent by the people
of Canada for blitzed London kids. They were like butterscotch shells, made to
look like peanuts, and were filled with soft toffee and chopped nuts, packed in
long white boxes. [10]

BCH's supporters in America really swung behind the Settlement, and they raised significant sums of money for the project to convert the bombsite of No 380 and the adjacent flats into a playground.

This now-battered photo, sent to BCH in January 1941,
has written on the back "Here is a picture of the doll
which made $200 for the Settlement on New Year's Day.
Love to you all, Cath."

BCH

Summer 1942: the nursery children enjoy the playground,
some months before the official opening...

BCH

23 September 1942: Mrs Winant, wife of the American Ambassador,
officially opens the playground created from the bombsite
with funds from the British War Relief Society of America.

BCH had a string of distinguished visitors during the war, not least Her Majesty the Queen on 8 July 1942, which was reported in the *Fulham Chronicle*:

Although the public knew nothing of the intended visit the news of the Queen's arrival soon spread, and hundreds of people assembled outside the Settlement ... The Queen was greatly interested in the playground, which has been constructed on the site of bombed buildings.

Here the Queen met Miss Sybil Baber JP, who recently retired from the position of Warden of the Settlement. Miss Baber told the Queen how members of the staff and herself were trapped for several hours under the wreckage when the Settlement was hit by a bomb during a raid in 1940. The Queen congratulated Miss Baber on her escape ... The Queen constantly expressed her pleasure at the brightness of the centre and said what impressed her most was its individualistic and friendly characteristics which made it so different from the ordinary institution ... As Her Majesty left the nursery the children shouted "Good-bye, King and Queen!" The Queen was very touched by this demonstration and said the King would be delighted to hear how he was greeted in his absence. [11]

Very soon after the bomb at No 380, an offer had come from the large and relatively new parish of Ruislip in Middlesex for BCH to form a sub-settlement. Many Fulham families had been evacuated there and the vicar, the Rev[d] A. A. Gorbold, had only himself and another male worker to handle a mass of parochial work. With the blessing of the diocesan authorities, two BCH workers moved to Ruislip, two more women were appointed there, and Miss Baber kept an oversight from Fulham. The vicar, reporting to BCH subscribers a year later, was delighted and not a little relieved at the impact made by the BCH arrivals:

Miss Exham has had a position of great responsibility at South Ruislip Mission Church. She has very largely had the leadership of the congregation in all its branches. Miss Codd has exercised an increasingly effective leadership in the work among children and adolescents, and has managed the sacristy with unobtrusive efficiency. Miss Joseph has not only led the Women's Fellowship, shared in Confirmation preparation, but has been in herself an intellectual stimulus of the greatest value. In addition to the management of the household she has accomplished a great deal of social work. Miss Monks, in starting the Ruislip Manor Youth Club, has been faced with a task that might well have broken anybody's heart. She has come to the end of her first year with a smile. It has been hard work and to some extent lonely work, for we are determined to be loyal to the club's undenominational character. The great response has been a reward to her efforts. [12]

Writing of the Youth Club, later in the same pages, Miss Monks reported:

We have socials (average attendance 120), a play-reading group, art class, first-aid class, and the girls have a keep fit and the boys a PT group ... Sunday nights are given up to debates and discussions. Sometimes as many as 70 boys and girls attend. Some of the subjects have been as follows: 'Equal Rights and Pay for Women,' 'Sunday Opening of Cinemas,' 'The Function of the Churches Today,' 'A Parson's Job,' 'Co-Education,' etc. [13]

After three years, the Ruislip sub-settlement had 'grown up' and could detach itself from BCH; Miss Codd had married one of the curates, and the various clubs now stood on their own two feet, under the management of the Ruislip Northwood Youth

Committee. In saying goodbye, the Annual Report for 1943-44 noted, "We cannot feel that a link so strongly welded can ever be broken, and the wise counsel of the Revᵈ A. A. Gorbold will often be asked for." [14]

...

There was another safety-valve away from London; Fendly House in Hertfordshire was offered to BCH by its owner, Mrs Fyleman, a former Care Committee worker, when she heard about the renewal of the blitz in early 1944:

> Within a week of this offer we had installed three infirm old ladies;
> the oldest is 90, and she has twice had her home destroyed by enemy action;
> three girls without mothers and one mother with her little girl, and one
> other friend willing and able to run the house ... It is a very old converted
> farm house which offered to us such a warm welcome from the start that
> we want to rechristen it 'Friendly House.' [15]

But these small blessings could not be spread to all, and back in Fulham, as the war drew into its fifth year, strains were beginning to tell. The work of the School Care Committees was increasingly difficult as more and more parents were out working all day and evening visits, in the blackout, were at least laborious and sometimes hazardous. But there was also a subtle change in the children of the borough:

> Many of us are concerned about the increasing 'rowdiness' which is apparent
> in the behaviour of the young people of today. Even our smallest Nursery
> School child attempts to compete with the Luftwaffe in the noise of his playful
> bombing operations. This desire for noise is not confined to play, but is
> demonstrated in their behaviour on the streets and in public places. Some
> people are inclined to pass it over as a war-time condition. That may be so,
> but we must take care that our own organisations do not tend to increase this
> tendency, which may be accentuated by living in crowds. [16]

And over the page, the problem was analysed further:

> There is increasing a new form of child neglect. We hear from Care
> Committee workers, from CAB officers, and from all who work with
> mothers and children, complaints that mothers have not time to give to their
> children. No, they are not dirty, and they are not underfed, but they do lack care
> and attention. Few mothers have time to accompany a child to a medical
> inspection, fewer have time to take the child for dental treatment, and fewer
> still have time to play with their children. One mother was heard to boast that
> she could get rid of her little girl and the baby for five hours for sixpence, if they
> sat through two performances at the cinema! This breaking up of the family is a
> serious thing, and we have to remember these facts to those who would
> encourage mothers to continue going out to work after the war. This, too, has
> been one of the costly wartime emergencies and it is a fallacy to say "It worked
> all right during the war." [17]

BCH kept its clubs going, even through the Flying Bomb menace, and there were some occasions for pride; early in 1944, Dr Kraus, the Foreign Minister of the Czech government in exile, offered through the International Youth Council to present radio sets as prizes to the five youth clubs in Britain who could demonstrate work in contributing to the war effort and furthering international relations. BCH took up the challenge with almost manic zeal:

> We did all forms of service such as club members spending one night a week
> in Fulham Hospital, knitting for the Merchant Navy, collecting books for a

Barrage Balloon Unit, collecting for the Red Cross, running a football match and giving the proceeds to [illegible]. Then on the international side we organized an International Exhibition which the ex-Mayor of Narvik opened, had an International Concert, an International Party, an International Ramble and an International Brains Trust with speakers from many different countries. Our main object was to put any money that we collected into a big fund so that we could buy a raft for the Merchant Navy. We succeeded in collecting £50, which was our target. [18]

After all that, how could Dr Kraus *not* give BCH Club one of the five radio sets. The magazine *Youth News* described the prize-giving:

One Friday evening in September we made our way to Fulham to the grand celebration dance which accompanied the presentation of the radio set to Bishop Creighton House. The dance band had a rival that night for the siren wailed forth at least three times. But the uncomfortable near bumps of a couple of doodlebugs served only to remind us of the extra strain which London youth has faced with courage - perhaps their greatest contribution to the national war effort. BCH has a very fine international record, and it was mainly their work in furthering friendships with young people of other countries and helping where they could that brought them to the forefront in this contest. Dr Kraus, presenting the set, referred to the great part the BBC has played during this war in strengthening the determination of the peoples of Europe to resist. He thought the radio could play an increasingly important part in linking the ideas of young people in different countries after the war. Both members of parliament for Fulham, Dr Summerskill and Mr Astor, were present for the ceremony which was presided over by the Mayor. [19]

For some young people the transition to adulthood took place during the war. Jim Smith, who had broadcast to America as Vice-President of the Youth Club in 1941, been a useful stopper centre half in the BCH football team, and played the drums as accompaniment to the blues piano of the Rev[d] Tatton Arundel at Club dances, joined the Merchant Navy in 1943 and served the rest of the war on convoys to Norway. Even there though, BCH kept in touch, and over sixty 'old boys' in the forces received regular newsletters about Club activities, and parcels of goodies to ease, in Jim's case, the bitter conditions of life in the Arctic Ocean. The men wrote back in gratitude, and it was clear their thoughts were turning to the post-war world:

When I first came into the Army it made me realise what benefits can be derived from the clubs that are made for the use of the Servicemen and women and although I didn't realise so much when I was in civilian life that we really needed clubs like the BCH for good companionship and friendliness that is needed in these days and I see no reason why the club should not be kept running after the war but maybe on a bigger scale. [20]

***

FRIDAY NIGHTS.

Babies in prams can be left at the Green Tree from 6-30—10 o'clock, to give young parents a chance to go out together.

MEMBERSHIP.

This will be open to all parents and children of Adeney Road, who subscribe towards the upkeep and development of the House.

Children 1d. per meeting.
Adults 6d. per week.

THE GREEN TREE.

THE GREEN TREE HOUSE on the corner of Adeney Road, is put at the disposal of the Children and Parents of the Road.

ITS AIM IS :-

To provide them with a centre for play and occupation.

To promote their well-being, by furthering their health and education.

To foster a happy community spirit.

Children will meet in groups twice weekly.

I. 2—5 years old.
II. 5—9 years old.
III. Over 9 years old.

The House will always be open to parents and it is hoped that parents will join in the children's activities and also will form groups among themselves for recreational and educational purposes.

BCH

The front and back of a small card,
slipped through the letter-boxes of every house
in Adeney Road in September 1946.

THE GREEN TREE

"The first rule the children proposed was that standing
on tables should not be allowed."
Report on Green Tree House [1]

This is a short sad story. It illustrates in microcosm how a good idea, born of careful thought, conscientiously carried out and with support on all sides, can nonetheless flounder and die, helpless in the face of a complication arriving out of nowhere.

As World War Two came to an end, BCH was more than ever troubled by the dislocation of family life the war had brought about, and especially its effect on children:

> Children seemed destructive far beyond the degree which is appropriate to youth. It was much more difficult than up to 1939 to get them to see why they should not pilfer or practice minor fraud. The moral significance of these tendencies has been sharpened by the economic straits in which our whole community is now living. [2]

> One of the main difficulties in the way of improving these conditions for childhood in London was the apparent lack of parental interest. Few mothers and fathers seemed to understand that they had any necessary part in their children's activities. This limits children's intellectual and emotional development to an extent for which there is no adequate compensation. Evacuation and the war's effect in breaking up family relationships, which in so many cases had now to be built all over again, all contributed with over-crowding to produce these results. [3]

In response to this situation, BCH evolved the idea of finding a house in Fulham, ideally near BCH, but separate and distinct, which could be devoted to the children of the immediate neighbourhood; it should be *their* house, they should develop house activities, house rules and in so doing they would come to cherish the place as theirs, and, it was hoped, begin to appreciate the value of joint property in the wider community. This house, it was thought, should be a secure environment for the children, would be an escape from the crowded conditions at home, and would give them a structured liberty in which to engage with their peers. It was also hoped, of course, that the parents too would take an interest, and the house would be a catalyst to improved family life. The search for premises was begun, and approaches for support made to the borough and the LCC.

A house was found four hundred yards down Lillie Road: 334a was a former coffee shop, with a basement and two floors of accommodation above, somewhat the worse for wear since the next door house was destroyed by enemy action, and uninhabited for the past two years. But it could be had for a rent of £90 per annum, plus £50 rates. The Fulham Children's Council supported the proposal and a fund of £500 was assembled; £200 from an anonymous donor for equipment and the major share coming from the Lord Mayor's Air Raid Distress Fund. In October 1945 BCH agreed with the Fulham Children's Council to set up a joint committee of management, though ultimate financial responsibility would remain with BCH. In the light of other commitments, and not wishing to embark on an indefinite journey into the unknown, it was agreed the experiment should last in the first place for one year, and then be reviewed. Putting the house in order proved to be rather a saga; new structural problems surfaced as the work progressed, then at quite a late stage the LCC surveyor decided that a whole range of safety measures were necessary if the house was to be occupied by children. Finally, very late, it was found that the earth banked against the side wall after the demolition of the next door house produced so much dampness in the basement rooms that a whole new round of work had to be undertaken to make them usable. The last straw was a break-in by a local gang who vandalised the interior and smashed up the toys already collected. All these additional blows threw the budget into disarray, and BCH was grateful, when they approached the LCC Education Committee for supplementary help, to get an agreement that they would give substantially towards the house organiser's salary.

The search for the right person to run the house led eventually to Fraulein Friedl Kruse, and the decision to appoint her opened a flurry of letters to and fro with the Home Office and other bodies, because there had just been a war and she had been interned. [4] She was 35, had a German social-pædagogical diploma, and had come to England in 1936 after problems with the Gestapo. Before the war she had worked with maladjusted children through the Parents' Institute under Professor Charlotte Bühler. Although classified as a 'friendly alien' she was interned in the general round-up of 1940, had spent the war teaching in the internment camp school and was only released in early 1945. But she was able to muster glowing references, and eventually her clearance came through, and BCH could officially bring her on board. It was at her suggestion, early on, that the name 'Green Tree House' was adopted for the project.

334a Lillie Road stood at the corner with Adeney Road, which no longer exists, the area having been built over and re-laid out with the coming of the Bayonne Road Estate. Given that the project was founded on the notion of intensive work with a small group it was decided that Green Tree House would be exclusively for the sixty children of Adeney Road, and Miss Kruse would have constant difficulties turning away children from other nearby streets - with help later, it should be said, from the Adeney Road kids, who had become proud of their place.

One of Miss Kruse's first tasks was to undertake a micro-sociological examination of the community in Adeney Road, which gives a fascinating insight into the structure of neighbourhood relationships, and evokes a small Fulham landscape of yesteryear that might seem almost pre-historic viewed from the world of 2008:

> Adeney Road is divided into upper and lower parts by a bend in the road.
> The grocery shop at this bend is a common meeting ground, as families from
> both ends do their shopping there. A larger proportion of children come from
> the lower end; twenty-five families with thirty-nine children of school age, also

twelve children over and six under school age. All, with the exception of two families have only one floor of a small house. In the upper part are fourteen families with twenty-two children of school age, plus two older and five babies. The houses here are larger, and even if shared are more self-contained, as there are separate lavatories and the upper floors have water laid on. Neighbourhood-consciousness is divided into two loosely-knit self-contained groups; the people of the two ends seem hardly to know each other. This manifests itself as soon as the slightest quarrel springs up between the children, they divide at once into two camps. On the occasion of the VE [Victory in Europe] Day Party, which was being arranged by the whole street and held in the lower part, the children from the upper end said they had not been nicely treated and had not had their fair share. In consequence the VJ [Victory in Japan] Day Party was arranged for the upper end by their parents and for them only, a fact which is still often referred to by the lower end children. [5]

Miss Kruse opened Green Tree House with a deliberate lack of ceremony on 30 September 1946. Almost all the children in the road came on the first day, but worryingly only seven mothers bothered to turn up. When the dust had settled, her report continued:

> After the first eight weeks the children had grasped the idea that the 'Green Tree' really was their own house. By that time they had recovered from their initial surprise that the organizer did not start them off with games or tell them what to do. They raced wildly through the house with the greatest possible noise or settled down in the most unlikely places. They were delighted with every bit of occupational material when it came, like raffia, chalk, paint and paper. They were at liberty to do whatever they liked with the limited material available, or just to run around the house and invent their own games. The big downstairs room, especially after it had been covered with linoleum, gave particular pleasure to the 9+ age group, who played very active self-invented games or just 'let off steam.' With the minimum of supervision they arranged their own simple team games and usually avoided quarrels, although the smaller ones had sometimes to be protected from bullying. [6]

One curious area of friction arose with the small handful of boys who had already had some experience of organized junior clubs:

> This group responded very slowly to any suggestion to invent games and felt that there was little to do. After the arrival of table tennis facilities at Christmas they only came in to play this game. They requisitioned three of the four available tables, cleared all other children out of the room and settled down to play. When the organizer told them that the other children could not be expected to stop using the tables, they became very annoyed and began to annoy everybody … On another occasion during March, they took away all the shoes of all the boys playing in the large room and threw them into the snow in the yard. When they were told that the boys could not go into the snow in their socks to retrieve them, and that such behaviour was not funny at all, they complained that the rest could not understand a bit of fun. They brought the shoes in only very reluctantly. All the other children said they only came in to bully. On being told that such behaviour would not be tolerated in the house, these three boys rushed out, and have not come in since … This kind of attitude was lacking in boys without previous club experience. [7]

Cleansed of the disruptive element, the children developed their exploitation of the house even further:

> The 9+ age group enters the house on the whole with a pre-planned idea of what they are going to do. They have rehearsed and presented to the others their own little shows, and have done a lot of improvised acting. They have used the house for their own parties, for which they cooked and baked themselves. They had and still have fights and quarrels which always show immediately the division of the road into two parts. They often bring their own toys, boxing gloves or games to the house. On the whole the children turn towards the house as a place where they can go and do things they like and find a grown-up friend with whom they can discuss subjects which interest them. The improvement the linoleum gave the house impressed the children immensely. They themselves insisted that nobody should play in shoes on it, unless they had rubber soles. This rule the children enforce themselves. They consider the linoleum a valuable possession and are careful not to damage it. [8]

Discipline in Green Tree House was almost entirely self-imposed:

> The first rule the children proposed was that standing on tables should not be allowed … They further decided that after two warnings a child should be suspended for a week for minor trouble-making and two weeks for being rude. Swearing was thought to be a reason for being suspended without warning, and one of them added, "Of course, we all swear a lot, but not here." Lew, whose behaviour had been the reason for the meeting, was suspended for a week. Although his best friends asked after two days for him to be let back in, it needed not much reminder by the organiser of their own group decision. His friends agreed that Lew had 'asked for it.' During the suspension, Lew brought his younger brother to the door each day, and came back himself after the week in the best of moods. There has been no suspension since. [9]

The only disappointment was the attitude of the parents, who seemed to regard the house simply as a convenient place to offload their children, without taking up the invitation to get involved themselves:

> Before the house was ready for the children, all the parents were visited. Almost all of them showed great interest. It was explained to them that their active co-operation would be very much appreciated and that it was hoped they would come to the house while their children were there. And they were welcome to form groups among themselves. The fathers were very helpful with the laying of the linoleum, and they often enquire after things at the house, but they are still unreceptive to the overall idea. They frequently say they had all the community life they could ever wish for while they were in the army. It proved very difficult to arrange any meetings for the mothers, as they all work away from home, at least for part of the day. Individual mothers tried hard to spare the time to come to the house for a sewing class or a talk. They were willing to help to raise money for the house and suggested whist drives, or a jumble sale, but families in the road had hardly anything to turn out. On the whole the response of the parents has been very poor, although the organiser spent a considerable time in contacting them. They are friendly enough towards the house, but most of them take the view that 'They' - meaning the LCC - ought to be responsible for keeping the children off the streets. [10]

Miss Kruse had a sounding board at the regular meetings of the Green Tree House Management Committee, made up of representatives of BCH and the Fulham

Children's Council. A member of that committee had a shrewd understanding of the parents' attitudes:

The shelter life during the war years has given them so much community living that they are now almost anxiously guarding their privacy. As one man told me: "We are in a way like people who never think of God unless they are in a tight spot, then they pray - so we never think of the help we can give our neighbours unless we know they are in danger, or we ourselves need help, and have to call on people." [11]

The Report from which the above quotations are extracted was put together for the BCH Council after seven months of Green Tree's life. Miss Kruse had undertaken a complex experiment and thus far it had been successful; there seems never to have been any suggestion that her being a German was a problem, either with the children or with the parents. Her Report concluded:

Under the present economic conditions and with present-day housing problems, a house like Green Tree may be the place where children can really work out their own ideas and learn by their mistakes. It would probably need four to five years to arrive at firm conclusions about an experiment like this. It would almost take that time, it is felt, to secure the effective co-operation of the parents. It would be interesting to see the present 7-10 year-olds in adolescence and compare them with other adolescents from similar environments who had not had the benefit of such a house. [12]

Miss Kruse presented her findings to date to the BCH Council in March 1947 and was enthusiastically commended for the achievements so far. Though the expenses were going up a bit, it was felt this was nothing to be alarmed about, and Council unanimously voted an extra £50 immediately. Council was also gratified to learn that the parents had become more interested since the report was compiled.

But three months later came the unexpected blow, "It was unanimously felt that it would be a great pity for the house to close now but the owner had refused to let it for only another year and Miss Wickham, as one of the Trustees, refused to sign for so long a time as fourteen years." [13]

This was the crux: the owner would only grant a fourteen year lease, and would not contemplate an extension for just a year. For their part, BCH Council felt they could not enter into such a long term commitment. Mrs Pollard, of the Green Tree Management Committee, was asked to explore whether the house could be legally sub-let, if BCH were to sign up to the fourteen year lease and the experiment lapsed. At the next Council she reported that she had approached several bodies, without success, for further financial support. The Council reluctantly concluded, "The house would not be closed down because it had failed in its purpose, but because the financial position of Voluntary Bodies was so uncertain that the Council could not face taking a thirteen year lease on Green Tree House, the landlord having refused to entertain a shorter one." [14]

By the September meeting of the Council, the end had come:

Green Tree House was now closed and Miss Worster said that Miss Kruse taking the children to camp made a fitting conclusion to the year's experiment.

A certain Mr Martin wanted the house and was willing to relieve BCH of the last month of the lease ... Miss Kruse was still in possession of the flat and the Hon Secretary was asked to write her a strong letter pointing out that the accommodation went with the job, which had terminated on 31 August, and requesting her to vacate the premises immediately. [15]

One last postscript came up at the next meeting:

Miss Kruse was still in possession of the flat, but as the BCH tenancy had now expired there was nothing further to be done. Mr Martin had been written to asking for £50 in respect of fixtures installed by BCH. [16]

***

SOCIAL REVOLUTION

> "In the minds of many there has arisen lately a question
> as to the future of work such as ours..."
> BCH Annual Report 1949-50 [1]

When World War Two ended, and Clement Attlee's Labour Party won a landslide victory in the first post-war election, it was plain that a programme of social legislation was going to be enacted on a scale not seen since the days of Campbell-Bannerman and Asquith, the last Liberal Prime Ministers, at the time of BCH's birth. Writing in the first post-war Annual Report, the Chairman, Lady Gwen Moberly, sought to see ahead to where this tide of state takeovers was going to leave Settlements:

> So deeply has human need penetrated the consciousness of us all that, though we welcome thankfully the efforts of the State to meet it, we feel also that it is the job of Settlements to fill in the gaps, to watch the effects of these new measures and to oil the wheels of the necessary social adjustments - in short, to meet the needs of the citizen as an individual over and above the needs of the individual as a citizen. We are in a difficult transition stage ... Perhaps the drive towards social security is not the whole story and may put the emphasis too heavily on material and intellectual satisfactions. [2]

Many pre-war features of BCH life were resumed much as before; the Women's Holiday Fund, the Children's Country Holiday Fund and the BCH Youth Clubs all started again going places where they had left off in 1939, the latter not wholly without complications, as an unusually detailed report of the 1947 Youth Club camp on a farm at Mullion in Cornwall reveals:

> One of our main difficulties at camp was that our age range was too wide, we had boys and girls from the age of 14 to 21. Some of our seventeen and eighteen year olds think that they cannot have a good time without having a good drink. A party of club members went to the pub at Mullion early on in the camp, two of them had too much to drink, and one of them was a girl of fifteen. The publican rang me the next day, and the pub was banned for the rest of the camp. This was a good action on the part of the publican, and all the club members felt the disgrace. Two nights after this three or four of the members when to a pub at a village some four miles away, but they did not have too much to drink. Our other main difficulty was a Sailors' camp near Helston, some of our girls met these sailors at a dance and were escorted home by them. We only had this trouble in the first week, because the most difficult girls concerned returned home at the end of the first week. The three most troublesome boys also returned home at the end of the first week. Out of the 45 members at camp it was only a small proportion who caused the trouble in the village. The other club members thoroughly enjoyed themselves, they had never

before been to country as beautiful as Cornwall, they loved the sea, they loved the farm, they would watch the milking and even try milking themselves, and there was great excitement when a calf was born. [3]

If the statistic was available, it would surely show that the average age of BCH's 'customers' has steadily gone up over the whole hundred years, and more especially since World War Two. As the state and the borough have taken over more and more of the provision for children and young people, BCH has turned its attention more and more to that growing and relatively neglected sector, the old.

BCH

**Summer 1949: A party of BCH Club members setting off
for a fortnight's holiday.**

The elderly are more likely to be housebound and bedridden and lonely than any other group, and therefore less readily able to take advantage of the club life at BCH. Realising this, an initiative was started in early 1949 of visiting old folk at home. It was the idea of Miss Lilian McCulloch, who had first volunteered as a young girl at BCH as long ago as 1921, when she helped with the infants and was for a time secretary of the Ruridecanal Council for Youth. She had then moved to Torquay for most of her adult life, but now, in middle age, she was back in Fulham, and once more throwing her energies at the disposal of BCH. In starting the visiting, and gathering a group of eight volunteers for the task, she was plainly tapping a great need, and she evidently brought a quality of selflessness to the task that could not fail to impress:

Miss McCulloch heads up all our work for the welfare of old people
in Fulham and provides the inspiration to all her helpers. She is always
at the beck and call of all those who need her or who are in any sort of trouble.
When an old person who is bedridden falls out of bed, someone flies to Miss

McCulloch for assistance, if an old man is without fuel, it is she who sees some is delivered quickly, if someone is taken ill Miss McCulloch never ceases until some hospital can be persuaded to receive the patient. She visits at homes or hospital untiringly, begs bed jackets, nightdresses, warm pyjamas and vests for her old friends, and usually takes them herself to hospital - waiting till they are comfortably settled in before leaving them - or to their convalescent home. It was she who made all the arrangements for the infirm and housebound to be conveyed to the Mayor's Boxing Day Party, and in spite of all our protests she pays out of her own pocket for countless little needs. [4]

The visiting could sometimes produce heartwarming results:

One of our visitors, finding that her old lady was very sad at never having heard from her son in Canada for over thirty years, took immense trouble in trying to find his whereabouts, and finally wrote to the Mayor of the town where he had last been heard of. She succeeded in tracing him and consequently the old mother has been overjoyed at getting letters from this son again. [5]

There was also 'Case Work' which 'is a somewhat grandiloquent title given to the work of making friends with difficult people.' [6]

There are always the people who seem unable to help themselves or to cope without a great deal of encouragement and guidance … We have our quota in Fulham and a worker may have to do lengthy daily visits over a long period of time before even the tiniest result is shown. One such is Mrs X. She is of low mentality and is married to a man who bullies her. She has four children, the eldest 8 years old, and she is expecting another in May. She lives in a two roomed flat and is quite incapable, spiritually, mentally or physically, of coping with life and her family. She must have a friend, someone always about and ready to put up with her bad ways as well as her good. This is an NSPCC family and we all agree that the best possible way to help her is to get her sent to a Rehabilitation Centre after the new baby is born. In the meantime she needs constant visiting and practical help; the real creative work will only begin when she returns home after her time at the Rehabilitation Centre.

Stories of these families could fill a book, but we must end by telling you an incident which may not be complimentary but which pleased the Case Worker enormously: A Problem Mother said to her, "I hear you went to see Mrs A the other day, love, and she didn't ask you in! She told me she was in an awful muck and didn't like to, and I tells her never to mind about you, for you was one of us, and it never mattered what muck you was in." [6]

In that same Annual Report there were reviews of all the various activities BCH undertook; taking in and teaching students on attachment, the Junior Boys' Club, the Junior Girls' Club, the Youth Club, a newly-formed Young Adult Club, the Women's Fellowship (BCH's longest-running club, Christian based, started in 1935), the Old People's Clubs (not only at BCH but also at St Andrew's Hall, West Kensington), the Play Centre...

Summer 1953: The Play Centre children on a day trip to Chesham Bois.

1951: The 'Young Mums' watch a demonstration.

... the Young Mothers' Fellowship, better known as the 'Young Mums', the Hospital Club (newly-begun in January 1953, an endeavour to alleviate, by visiting, the apathy and inertia of the chronic sick wards at Fulham Hospital), the Olde Tyme Dancing Club, the Blind Clubs, the Fulham Social Workers' Lunch Club (a monthly gathering to hear invited speakers on topics of current concern such as 'Play Therapy', 'Church work among refugees' and 'The Invalid Children's Aid Association'), the Southern Chapter (a discussion group of Women Church Workers), the Poor Man's Lawyer (a weekly evening session with 125 applicants in the year 1952-3), Children's Care Committees (BCH had members on these committees at eight local schools), the Women's Holiday Fund and the Children's Country Holiday Fund. But no more clinics, the last had left in 1950, and there was a recognition that the social landscape around BCH had changed dramatically:

> The people themselves are very different from those of even twenty
> years ago. One rejoices to see the smart mums at a school medical, purring
> proudly over young Michael and Anna, chock-full of vitamins, school dinners,
> milk and malt! The Settlement is no longer the one brightness in their lives;
> there is television, LCC-financed Play Centres and Recreational Institutes,
> cheap dance halls, cinemas, good money and adequate holidays for almost
> everyone. Troublesome children are no longer smacked but sent to the Child
> Guidance Clinic, and it all means the Welfare State is here. [7]

A long way indeed from the Fulham of the 1930s, memorably evoked by Jim Smith in our interview; "If you paid your rent two weeks in a row, the police came round to see where you'd got the money from." [8] The BCH Report continued:

> This is good and thank God the old grinding poverty has gone, but
> something else has gone too. The people are no longer individuals, each
> 'the unrepeatable experiment of God,' but numbers on case papers filed
> into an interminable filing-box; and Social Workers, each a highly trained
> specialist, pursue them with tireless energy, seizing on a Problem Family
> with the enthusiasm of a butterfly collector on a Purple Emperor ... Possibly
> the Settlement of the future should be a Bethany where a few active clubs are
> run. (How can we compete, and why should we, with the Evening Institute,
> Dance Hall and Television?). It may be a home to which the tired, the defeated
> and the depressed, the sinful and the joyous can come, and see in those there
> the sympathy, gentleness, utter self-forgetfulness of our Blessed Lord Himself. [7]

Ceding ground to new competition was of course nothing new: in the 1930s, BCH had run a series of Sunday evening concerts by distinguished professional musicians in the Garden House, which had eventually been reluctantly discontinued, killed off, it was agreed, 'by the power of the wireless'. Similarly the Apprenticeship and Skilled Employment Committee, begun before World War 1 and revived in 1927, was closed down in 1938 in recognition of "The change in the conditions of the labour market which has resulted in very numerous vacancies for juveniles, together with the increasing efficiency of the Employment Exchanges ... have rendered unnecessary our duplication of the function of placing these boys and girls." [9]

As various activities were phased out - either through takeover, through moving elsewhere, or through declining interest - it was noted, in 1958, "We are letting many more rooms than we did." [10] This trend has continued to the present day, with some curious passing tenants along the way. In amongst long term customers, there were some who brought a certain perplexity, as the Warden reported to Council in June 1969:

A group of people called the 'Young Socialists' hired a room at BCH on one evening a week. They were completely untroublesome but a casual enquiry by the Warden had revealed that they had parted company with the Labour Party because they were too far to the left. When asked if they were Communists they had said that they were not because they disapproved of the Russian attitude in Vietnam [The Warden may have got hold of the wrong end of the stick here; Young Socialists disapproved of practically everything about Soviet Russia, except their stance on Vietnam]. The Warden had not been able to discover any more but felt that she must ask Council what it thought in view of the religious aspects of the Constitution which might apply to Communists or near-Communists. After some discussion Council decided that they should be allowed to continue their hiring of the room, as they seemed to be very harmless and serious-minded people, but on no account must they or any other political group use BCH as their postal address. [11]

And then later that year, "The Young Socialists had had difficulties in the late spring and early summer because of rowdy young people joining the group. They had handled this very well but in July had felt that they could not continue and had closed the club." [12] Along the way there have been tenancies by, among many others, the London School of Florists, SPIF (Single Parents in Fulham), Toc H, the Joanne School of Dancing, Age Concern, MIND and the Fulham Community Youth Theatre. The latest BCH Annual Report (for 2007) lists as 'some of the groups using BCH': Alcoholics Anonymous (5 sessions a week), Art Class, Breakaway, Community Education Forum, Community Housing & Therapy, Councillors' and MP's surgeries, Family Placement Unit, Hammersmith & Fulham Citizens' Advice Bureau, Hammersmith & Fulham Multi-Cultural Forum, Hammersmith & Fulham Primary Care Trust, Hammersmith & Fulham Refugee Forum, Hestia Housing, Iraqi Association, Japanese Calligraphy, Kixa Self-Defence, Mount Carmel, Narcotics Anonymous (2 sessions a week), NESBFA, OOT, Safety Net, Sahaja Yoga, SGI Lay Buddhist Organisation, Smart Training, Somali Children's Advocacy, Spiritist Psychology Society, SIRO Aid, Sudanese Development Association, VSRA, Weight Watchers (2 sessions a week), West London Mental Health Trust and the Youth Offending Team. While their collective rent payments are a vital part of BCH income, it must be accepted that these organisations have no special loyalty to BCH, and in an area where all sorts and sizes of offices and halls are available to hire, they can easily move on if better or cheaper spaces become available elsewhere. Of course, another way of looking at this proliferation of small single-issue independent groups is that their growth is a tribute to BCH's encouragement of the self-help ethic; it calls to mind one of Samuel Barnett's comments; 'A healthy charity exists to destroy itself'.

March 1951: rebuilding of No 380 at last gets under way.
The eleven year wait since the bomb fell is a reminder of the
difficulties and austerity of post-war conditions.
The trio at the front door may be Kathleen Worster, the Warden,
Arthur Moberly, the Hon Architect, and George Jones, the builder.

***

1968: 'The Mopeds' rehearse. "Complaints by neighbours about the noise have continued but the problem is likely to be solved as a result of a suggestion by the band itself - they will rehearse in the cellar."

YOUTH

"Particularly encouraging is the development in the Overseas Social Centre,
which inevitably has its own special difficulties to negotiate." [1]

In the run-up to BCH's fiftieth birthday there were various suggestions for special
'Jubilee' projects; one was concerned with 'the welfare of the coloured people now
living in Fulham.' [2] A club called the Overseas Christian Guild was formed and the
Warden reported to Council:

>The membership of this club is still mainly West Indian and English,
>although we have had visitors from many countries. Fenner Brockway [3]
>spoke one evening on 'The Challenge of the Coloured Man' and several
>Africans from the All Nations Club attended that night. Another evening
>we had an Egyptian, a Malayan, two Russians and a Frenchman. [4]

But whatever other exotic nationalities might have turned up from time to time in the
early days, the club swiftly became overwhelmingly West Indian, reflecting the
burgeoning population. In September 1958 the Rev[d] R. M. Campbell was assigned by
the Bishop of Jamaica, in an arrangement with the Society for the Propagation of the
Gospel, for one year to be the priest at BCH for West Indians. During his year at BCH
he broadcast an appeal on the BBC, and no doubt did useful pastoral work, but by the
time he returned to the West Indies the club had changed its name to the Overseas
Social Centre, abandoning the religious element in its original name.

In January 1960 the club held a successful first dance but Council noted with regret
that "those who come to the dances do not regularly attend the ordinary meetings of
the club." [5] By the end of the year, BCH had recognized that it needed something of a
rethink, "The Warden said that perhaps the OSC would best fulfil the need of its
members if it provided a place where they could meet casually to chat, without the
more formal and 'intellectual' type of programme hitherto arranged." [6]

Meanwhile, despite the conscientious efforts of many organisations including BCH,
there was no doubt that racial attitudes were hardening. The Warden reported to
Council that, "Problems with landlords and tenants had recently been arising in
Fulham and a BCH resident had been doing some visiting where the problem was
racial." [7]

Early the next year the OSC held a dance at Fulham Town Hall which was deemed a
success though it made a small financial loss, but in the aftermath BCH received a
disturbing letter from the Town Clerk of Fulham,

>complaining of damage to the piano and breakages and 'promiscuous behaviour'
>at the dance. It was agreed the Club should discharge its financial responsibilities

and the Warden had written to enquire the exact nature of the damage complained of. She had also questioned the truth of the last charge: Mrs Hanmer and Miss McIntosh had both been present and noticed nothing wrong and such behaviour was completely out of character and contrary to the usual social behaviour of the West Indians. [8]

BCH protested to the Town Clerk and, under detailed scrutiny, he withdrew his allegations. His claims had been, perhaps, an early example of prejudice finding evidence that wasn't really there. Anyway, a month later Council was happy to hear that, "A satisfactory letter from the Town Clerk had been received by the Warden and relations between the Club and the Borough Council appeared to be greatly improved." [9] Nonetheless there was clearly an edginess in race relations; both sides tending to see stereotypes rather than the real people. Early in 1964, Council was told of a recent evening event, "Students from the School of Tropical Medicine & Hygiene had attended a meeting and a frank discussion had taken place about the reactions of West Indian immigrants on coming to this country." [10]

The club continued active through 1964, in spite of difficulties caused by the floating population, which meant members tended to come and go, then in early 1965 there was another sad note in Council minutes; "There appeared to be a difficulty about coloured students helping with Meals on Wheels. Council members expressed the hope that this would dissolve itself." [11]

By 1966, it was reported that the average weekly attendance at the OSC Club was 40, the great majority West Indians aged between 18 and 25. A note of anxiety re-enters Council minutes:

The average age of membership has fallen considerably and this has produced new problems which the Club Officers could see. It was, however, very difficult for them to handle these problems which called for a certain amount of experience and expertise. It might be necessary to become more ambitious in order to meet the present situation which was both a challenge and an opportunity. [12]

It was hoped that the growing awareness in the Borough of the need for integration would give support to the development of the Centre. [13]

The Club Committee still felt that the present membership did not take responsibility within the club as it should. There was a feeling in some quarters that it would benefit the OSC if a second room was made available so that older members could pursue activities not attractive to the younger members. [14]

It may be the clarity of hindsight, but a storm was brewing, and although, for most of 1967, the reports to Council about the OSC are short and no more than routine, there was plainly tension in the air, both within the West Indian club membership, and between some of them and BCH:

A problem at club meetings was that some younger members gambled when playing cards. Last week they had not given up when asked by the Chairman, who finally removed the cards. This had caused a fight and the Chairman had sent for the Police. It seemed that the Police had behaved very well. Council re-iterated their opinion that the OSC was a means of keeping in touch with these young people and that there was here an opportunity to meet a social need. The Borough Youth Committee had said the Club was to be congratulated on attracting a group of youngsters such as these and although it was a difficult job, they hoped the older members would keep up their efforts. [15]

Again, the next year, the reports to Council are mostly brief and there is a sense of breath being held. Then, "There had been an incident of racial feeling during the previous week but staff had spent some time talking to the two people mainly involved and felt they had succeeded in sorting things out." [16]

In early 1969, the situation began seriously to deteriorate:

Problems have arisen through the rehearsals of the two bands. It was not only a matter of available rooms; the vibration from one of the bands ruled out the possibility of some groups holding meetings immediately about them or nearby … considerable discussion … points made:
i) BCH would wish to support the bands in every possible way especially bearing in mind the present inflammatory atmosphere in the country as a whole.
ii) Now that one group was turning professional a business-like arrangement must be made.
iii) It was quite unnecessary to amplify except for a short testing period.
iv) Other clubs and groups using BCH must be considered. [17]
There were many new members from the Shepherds Bush area and these were regarded by older club members as a rough and upsetting element. Miss Lauterwasser now took their money as they arrived, the reason being that it meant she could thus see and make contact with everyone who came. Because of the extent to which she had been able to make friends and be accepted by the club members there had been several encouraging, though awkward, cases where she and BCH had been turned to for help with personal problems. [18]
OSC is giving trouble. Attendance had built up to 80 the previous week and it was still run as the members wished i.e. with subdued lighting and very loud music. This made it difficult to control, and was certainly more than Miss Lauterwasser could handle without competent help. A lot of rough-housing was taking place, some petty thieving, and pranks which were sometimes downright dangerous - the previous week some members had filled a can with petrol and set it alight on a wall near St Clement's Mansions. The Warden and Miss Lauterwasser had also smelt pot being smoked on the premises. The pot question worried everyone considerably, because of the legal implications, and the Warden had talks with Dr Troy, Medical Officer of Health, Major Care of the Salvation Army, and Dr Cameron … the neighbours were not unnaturally up in arms about all the troubles in the street after meetings.
Miss Lauterwasser had spoken at the previous club meeting and said that certain things would not be tolerated: (a) smoking pot on the premises, (b) thieving, and (c) rough behaviour in or around BCH. If any of these things happened the club would have to be closed forthwith. [19]

And duly in June the OSC was closed down, and Miss Lauterwasser left. After a break of a couple of months BCH decided to give it another go, this time bringing in an older West Indian, Mr Worrell, to supervise, and the OSC re-opened in September 1969. The first Council after the re-opening was given a cautious review of the restart:

It was too early to say how the Overseas Club would develop. Mr Worrell thought that a much more mixed programme was desirable but the members wanted more music and a compromise appeared to be inevitable. The first open meeting had gone well and the atmosphere on the whole had been good. There would almost certainly be 'teething problems' and some pressure on Mr Worrell. [20]

Mr Worrell found himself in an uncomfortable bridging position between the well-meaning of BCH and the unreachability of an alienated youth:

The apathy of the members was seen by Mr Worrell as a symptom of the unrest and dissatisfaction felt generally by coloured boys and girls. Discussion on this point indicated that the problem was widespread and several Council members felt that the insistence on loud music and dark rooms was symptomatic of the wish to withdraw from social pressures. [21]

By early the next year, Council was increasingly concerned at tensions between Mr Worrell and BCH, which seemed to focus on 'Dai' [pronounced 'Day'] Wilson, the Warden:

Council discussed the analysis of work which had been submitted by Mr Worrell ... It was obvious from this document that Mr Worrell was as unhappy about the situation as Council and the Warden were. Father Dawson had had two talks with him in an attempt to clarify the position and he reported to Council on the impressions he had retained from these conversations. He felt that Mr Worrell's attitude was more that of a club worker who happened to be based at BCH, rather than that of a member of the Settlement, but that although he probably found it easier to work in the narrower field that this implied he also resented it and seemed to feel slights where none had been intended. Certainly a whole tangle of misunderstandings had grown up and there was definitely a personality clash with the Warden, the latter possibly caused by the difficulty a West Indian might experience working under a woman. The Borough Youth Officer had reported to the Warden both verbally and by letter that Mr Worrell had been highly critical both of her and the Settlement when speaking to his office. It seemed to Council highly regrettable that Mr Worrell did not feel able to keep his criticisms within the four walls of the Settlement. He felt very strongly that he had been misled about the state of the OSC when he was going to take it over last September - he had expected a 'going concern' and had instead found that he must build it up from scratch. [22]

A sub-committee was set up to try to resolve the difficulties, but it failed and Mr Worrell was given three months notice. The club kept going in a revised format, and BCH's bafflement also continued:

The OSC is now called the Youth Club. Attendance was running at about 35-40, and consisted of both sexes and all colours and mostly of 13-16 year olds from the Gilliatt and Henry Compton Schools. They were very noisy and seemed not to want to do anything except dance or stand and shout at each other. Council agreed that there was no point in discussing whether this was right or not until Mr Worrell's successor in the club had settled in. [23]

In yet another reshaping the Youth Club became the Key Club, still with a majority black membership but now concentrating on the need for teenagers of a place to gather before mothers came home from work. By September 1971, worried at the fractious tendencies inherent in too great an age span, BCH had decided to restrict the age range to 11-14, with a specific quiet period for homework built into club hours. In a slightly sad coda to all BCH's efforts over fourteen years to answer the needs of the young black community, Mr Hadley, the Club Worker, reported:

> He maintained contact with the 16-20 year olds who had been club members until July 1971. The group had a definite identity and met daily in the Lillie Road recreation ground. He met them there and elsewhere and had been told they had not found another club to join ... These boys, mostly West Indian, now attended commercial discotheques which charged nightly entrance fees between 25p and 50p. [24]

And the *coup de grâce* came nine months later:

> The Warden reported that because a new and extended provision for teenagers' leisure was now available the [Staff & Policy] committee recommended that the Club should be run down at the end of July. Council agreed to this recommendation. [25]

...

BCH may be said to have taken a break to get its breath back on the Youth front, but by 1975 they had returned to the fray and were trying again with 'The BCH Youth Project.' This project was set up, with backing from the Inner London Education Authority Youth Committee, to establish youth clubs on three North Fulham estates. The idea was that a full-time youth worker, Chris Stratton, working out of BCH, would help these clubs into existence so that they could be run by the people of the estates themselves. Stratton's role, it was envisaged, would be advisory; how to get grants, how to organise stewarding, insurance, accounts, whether to split membership into juniors and seniors, whether those two groups should meet on separate nights, or at different times on the same nights, how to handle relations with the existing Tenants' Association. Clearly, some of the ambitions had a duality about them: the young people wanted a place that was, at least for one or two nights a week, theirs exclusively, on the other hand they wanted adult help and supervision, and, more subtly, they wanted adult approval and recognition. The particular stories of the clubs thus brought into existence are complicated and riven with the often Byzantine tensions of estate life where minor incidents can threaten to overturn months of careful work. For example:

> It had been decided previously by the Club Management Committee that the coffee bar should be run by the senior girls but this was not approved of by the Tenants' Association. However the coffee bar has continued to be run by the girls for some time and relations with the Tenants' Association helpers became tense. In March, the Club arranged a Disco with a rock band for the seniors and this was successful until the final minutes when an incident took place between the band's singer and a member of the audience. To complicate matters, the singer was the son of the adult Club organiser, he was drunk and hit the audience member with the microphone. He was taken home by his mother who said the Club was 'trouble' and that her husband was wasting his time in doing anything for the 'youths.' [26]

From the tone of Chris Stratton's reports it is clear that the majority of the adult population on all the estates tended to regard young people as a bit of a nuisance, and getting volunteers from among the adults proved difficult; when one or two did come forward, they all too often tended to fade away faced with the indifference or hostility of their neighbours. Nonetheless, some brave souls persisted:

> It needs to be remembered that the local adults are new to youth work and growing in their capacities as people, as youth workers and as club managers, and that their skills are limited. For example, in one club severe problems were caused for almost all the club personnel by the difficulty in responding to a group of educationally capable and articulate youngsters who manifestly wanted to have a more exclusive club. The local adults had difficulty in seeing their demands as being other than those of 'smart alecs' who 'fancied themselves.' [27]

Part, at least, of Chris Stratton's task was inculcating an understanding approach by both sides:

> [The Worker] has attempted to pass on simple human relations skills. For example, by refusing to feed into the gossip that surrounds a club and its life and instead encouraging people to say what needs saying to an appropriate person at an appropriate time. "Have you told him? Why don't you tell him?" is a response the worker may use in inviting an individual to take responsibility for his own views and behaviour. [28]

Subsequently further schemes along similar lines were launched in West Kensington and elsewhere in Fulham. By 1980, the Executive Committee were informed, nine youth clubs had been started, of which five at that time were still running.[29] BCH had worked with 48 volunteers and 12 part-time paid staff, it was felt that progress had been made in an intractable field. But this was a roller coaster; two years later there were "Serious problems! Disciplinary action in progress with full time worker. General work of the clubs falling apart ... low staff morale." [30] Yet by November, the Director could report things were back on an even keel with a full complement of full-time and part-time staff. [31]

By 1988, despite savage cuts in ILEA funding, the estate-based youth clubs had set up a mutual support federation among themselves, and they were now reliant wholly on volunteer workers from the estates rather than BCH workers. Now there was a flourishing branch of the Project at BCH itself about which the latest full-time worker, Quentin Charatan, reported in jocular vein:

> The Project is going far too well at the moment. It is far too popular, and attracting far too many young people. We can just about cope, but can the rest of the Settlement? To add to our difficulties they actually expect to <u>do</u> something when they're here, so we have to spend our time helping them with their homework, offering careers advice, doing art work, computer programming, going to the theatre, and God knows what else. [32]

Two years on and the roller coaster had dipped again; a Discussion Paper was put up to Council titled, 'Work With Young People at BCH - a New Direction':

> It has become apparent that resources for youth work will diminish significantly in BCH and throughout the Borough. We were cut by 33% two years ago and the full time vacancy may not be filled. This approximates a further cut of 21%... Initial discussions have taken place with representatives of the Borough Community Education Service and there are indications that the establishing of a youth education project could usefully be explored. The previous plans for

detached work had included substantial curriculum-based work so that the new direction is not too far distant from our original thinking. An educational bias would help us to:

> a) Give a clear direction within the ethos of youth work at BCH.
> b) Plan effectively, with time to do so.
> c) Clarify equipment and renovation needs.

… As well as activities that could be established relatively quickly (e.g. homework clubs, supplementary schooling) there would be the need to spend time planning various activities including individual packages of education and training. We would continue to offer counselling and advice and offering positive role models, particularly to young black men and women. We would want to re-establish detached work (e.g. offering particular activities on identified estates) and to continue and strengthen business development. We recognise that various things have to take place before this new direction can become a reality:

> 1) There have to be places where young people <u>want</u> to come in order to use facilities and resources.
> 2) Young people must be involved in the process of establishing the new direction." [33]

The paper goes on to list a number of technical/staffing questions that need to be addressed, and concludes:

> BCH has always had the ability to attract young people. It is seen as independent and able to respond effectively to the needs of young people. It is vital that we continue to offer an adequate response to younger users. It is not possible to do this within present structures and resources. We need to identify a process for change to continue to offer a service. The start of that process is to identify a new direction. [33]

After fifteen years the Youth Project was finally wound down in 1990. Writing in the Annual Report, the Director, Colin Barnes, could not avoid a note of sadness:

> The viability of the Youth Project as an independent provision is, we have reluctantly concluded, no longer possible … An intense amount of work has gone into establishing exactly what we should be doing. Plans were drawn up on the basis of what resources we thought we had. These resources were then 're-defined.' … The situation we faced was that we could run a small club, but not the Youth Project. We have decided that for the sake of the young people and the staff we would relinquish the management of the Project … It only remains to express our deepest gratitude to those workers, both full- and part-time, who have shown such commitment to young people in BCH. The closure of the Youth Project does not reflect on the quality of their work. It is a sign of the time. [34]

***

May 2002: the 'Busy Bees' with their latest handstitched quilt,
sold in aid of BCH for £400 within an hour of appearing in
the shop window of Messrs Harvie & Hudson, shirtmakers, of Jermyn Street.

- 15 -

WOMEN

"I don't say women are the same as men,
but I refuse to assume they are different."
Mandell Creighton [1]

The oldest-established club for women at BCH was the Women's Fellowship; this was a group founded by Miss Baber in 1935, with, at least initially, an explicitly Anglican agenda. So, for example, in 1937 they had talks on 'What Baptism Means to the Church of England', 'How We get Our Hymns', 'The Meaning of Confirmation', 'What Holy Communion Means in the Church of England', 'How to Teach Children to Pray'. And their minutes charmingly record a meeting addressed by Miss Baber:

Our Warden kindly gave us a talk on how mothers should learn children religion, so they can become good Christians. Mother should start learning them at different stages such as from 1 to 3 years learn them to rely on you, don't hit them one minute and love them the next, then from 4 to 7 years take them to church and explain it to them, and from 8 to 10 let them know why they do things, also let them read a text out of the Bible. [2]

The Annual Report for 1938 gave a picture of a thriving group:

Talks on the lives of 'great women' have a strong appeal, such as those on Dame Henrietta Barnett and Octavia Hill. Musical afternoons, play readings, costume talks, and services of a devotional kind, have all gone to make up a good year's programme ... Participation in the Annual Council Meetings and Services of the Diocesan Federation of Women's Meetings has helped the women to realise that they are taking part in a great movement for the raising of educational and spiritual standards. "It makes you feel as how you are never too old to learn." was overheard after a particularly interesting afternoon. [3]

Celebrating its twenty-first birthday in 1956, the club allowed itself a little boast:

The Fellowship has met regularly every Wednesday afternoon since its foundation; even the alarms and excursions of war never forced us to close down, though our numbers shrank at times almost to vanishing point. Now we have 54 members on our list, with an average attendance of 40 ... The weekly programmes have followed the more or less usual pattern, covering a wide variety of interests, including films, talks, demonstrations, socials and outings. Our links with All Saints' and St Augustine's Fellowship are as close as ever. There is perhaps no need to add that we were again responsible for the Grocery Stall at the Christmas Sale. [4]

It was still going strong ten years on, but the 1966 Annual Report had to acknowledge the passage of time: "The Women's Fellowship is our oldest club; its members, like the rest of us, grow older year by year so that now membership is drawn entirely from the over 60 age group ... It has stability, resilience and an understandable disinclination to change for fear of spoiling something which has been part of life for a long time." [5]

The Women's Fellowship would close in the end in 1997; at what was the last Council Meeting before BCH converted into a charitable company the Chairman announced, almost in passing, that after sixty-two unbroken years of Wednesday afternoon sessions, the Fellowship was closing down because of 'a decrease in the number of members.'

There had been other groups before the war, but they had tended to be based on a single activity such as 'Keep Fit,' Folk Dancing and Olde Tyme Dancing ('more men needed!'). The formation of other women's clubs really began after the war, first with the Young Mothers' Club in the autumn of 1951. Their opening contribution to the Annual Report evokes the time; "We generally have an informal social afternoon, arranging games of different kinds, the children in the meantime happily playing with toys. Two cookery demonstrations have been given by a representative of the North Thames Gas Board and we had a most interesting set of slides shown of life in Nigeria." [6] Running the club on behalf of BCH was one of the legendary figures in the Settlement's modern history, Miss Katharine Troutbeck, a resident from 1942 to 1958, who had been involved in the most difficult work immediately post-war of re-establishing family relationships fractured by evacuation, service in the forces or women's wartime work. There is a slightly out of focus photograph of her on the wall of the Liardet Room at BCH, and one would wish to know more about her. We are left with the charming faint impression of her given by Joyce Warmington in her talk to the Women's Club AGM in 2000: apparently Miss Troutbeck was given to walking around singing the song 'There was an Old Woman who Swallowed a Fly.' She died only a year after retiring from BCH and her obituary said "No one who came in contact with her could fail to be warmed by her large-hearted friendliness and unquenchable sense of humour." [7]

The group changed its name a couple of times, briefly calling itself 'The Young Wives', then 'The Young Mothers' Fellowship', but they were generally known as the 'Young Mums,' which sounds a bit more apt for the way they went about things:

It is a cheerful group and a very noisy one; it is certainly not intellectual, but as one Mum said, "It is good to get out of the house and have a good laugh" ... We had a good outing to Littlehampton in June, even if a large part of the day was spent in finding Woolworths in order to compare it with the ones in Hammersmith and North End Road. [8]

In amongst the games, the club, sometimes linking with other BCH groups, had a full range of guests speakers:

On make-up by Boots Ltd, on how to use the various gadgets on a sewing machine by Singer Ltd, on the care of the feet, particularly children's, by Dr Scholls Ltd. Mrs Palmer, from the staff of *Woman's Journal*, came to show us how to make Christmas decorations at home ... and recently a representative of Domestos Ltd brought an intriguing array of test tubes to demonstrate how different detergents react to different substances. [9]

In 1968, recognising that the membership no longer had pre-school children and were rather more these days talking about problems with adolescents, the club again changed its name, to 'The Women's Club.' Its contribution to the Annual Report glowed with pride:

> We are a robust, self-programming, outward-looking club … There are outside interests like 'International Help for Children' and the London Association of Women's Clubs. Members are personally involved in parent-teacher associations, scout groups and adult groups in other parts of the Borough. But their loyalty to and practical involvement in the life of BCH remains. Their support, whether with a social problem or in a money-raising effort can always be counted upon and the club is seen, not only as an integral part of our present life, but as a guarantee of our future. [10]

Forty years on, a world away now from young motherhood, the Women's Club members continue to be the hard core backbone volunteers for all those old-fashioned but irreplaceable activities of a charitable body; jumble sales, stalls at local fairs and fetes, turkey lunches, flag day selling, making Christmas cards, and the agenda for club nights remains as eclectic as ever:

> We had a Yeoman Warder from the Tower of London who gave us a most interesting talk on the Tower and the people - wives and children - who spend their lives in the confines of the Tower. He invited us to go one evening and see the 'Ceremony of the Keys' and we thoroughly enjoyed that. We also made a visit to a candlemaker and had a glassblower show us how to make ornaments and animals. [11]

There is one other women's group at BCH that must be accorded more than a passing mention; its history is older even than the Women's Club, and has involved more name-changes. Come back to the dark days of 1942; Miss Emmie Dodds, BCH's third Warden, writes in the Annual Report:

> The clothing problem of the poorer people is indeed acute at this time. These people had no reserve wardrobe when rationing was introduced (nor ever had), and the clothes they can afford to buy, though demanding the maximum value in coupons, give the minimum value of wear. Through the continued generosity of friends the clothes available at our Jumble Sales have been a great blessing to these people. To supplement this still further, we have started a 'Make Do & Mend' Class for mothers, where they learn to see a discarded frock coat as two pairs of shorts, and an old pair of trousers as a smart new skirt. [12]

The next year Miss Dodds could report on a lively going concern:

> The jolly crowd of younger mothers who come with their babies to 'Make Do & Mend' on a Thursday afternoon are not at all depressed by the fact that they have to mend and make do - and with Miss W. Talbot as their hostess it would be impossible for them to feel dull for a moment. The evening meetings were much disturbed by frequent alerts during the winter, and had to be suspended completely during the recent raids. [13]

There is a slight hiatus after the war, when this activity disappears from the minutes, but it re-surfaces in 1960 as the Tuesday afternoon 'Sewing Class'; "Members, under the leadership of Miss Tucker, never run short of ideas and interest. This informal group welcomes newcomers who wish to work in a friendly atmosphere." [14]

Over the next four or five years the group shifted back and forth between calling itself the 'Sewing Class' or the 'Craft Class', but whatever the name it continued to grow, and its Tuesday afternoon sessions continued to be described as 'lively.' By 1968, the 'Craft Class' had become officially a course of the Fulham & South Kensington Adult Education Institute, with a qualified teacher paid by the Inner London Education Authority. The Annual Report is a little amused:

> Supposedly members come to do needlework, to sew, to knit or crochet. Actually the group meets for social reasons as well. They enjoy meeting friends and the conversation is as important to them as their needlework. This fact is appreciated by the Principal of the Institute who recognises the educational value of social intercourse and arranges for us to have teachers who fit in well to the atmosphere of the group. [15]

When ILEA was abolished in 1990 there might perhaps have been a chance that the 'Craft Class' would have gone with it, but that would have been to reckon without Audrey Surtees. She thought, and so did the others, that these Tuesday afternoons were worth keeping going, teacher or no, and so the 'Busy Bees' came into existence. And there they are to this day in the Wickham Room on a Tuesday, knitting, sewing, crocheting, and Camilla makes the tea at 2.00 o'clock.

The Busy Bees' most impressive products over the nearly two decades of their existence have been a series of patchwork quilts, which have sold for anything up to £400, proceeds of course going to BCH. These quilts are made from odd off-cuts, some of which Audrey Surtees persuaded Messrs Harvie & Hudson, the shirtmakers, to donate. She then further persuaded them to display the finished products in their window, thus ensuring sales at good prices to the passing clientele of Jermyn Street. And to think this all started from wartime 'Make Do & Mend.'

**

WHAT ARE SETTLEMENTS FOR?

"No technical efficiency can supply entirely what is needed in a Settlement worker:
there must be a quality of spirit as well as of intelligence."
Miss Sybil Baber [1]

It would be fair to say that in BCH's first quarter of a century, no-one worried much
what Settlements were for; it was obvious, the needs were so great, there was so much to
do, let us get on with it. If the subject was debated, there is no record. But, by the
1930s, there had been a change in the landscape within which Settlements operated:
When Barnett founded Toynbee Hall, the educated men of the upper
classes were still the effective rulers of the world. They initiated new ideas.
They carried them out ... The reform movement at that time was pushed
forward by volunteers who to influence the experts had themselves to become
experts ... Since then there have been two great changes, due in no small
measure to the efforts of these pioneers. Firstly, the government itself has
armies of civil servants who are carrying out as officials the work of the social
reformer. Secondly, Labour and the Labour Party have grown up; they have
their own organisations, their own experts, their own lecturers who have actually
emerged from those strata of life which the Toynbee pioneers set themselves to
explore. So successful was the University Settlement movement that, in its
original form, it has ceased to be necessary. [2]
Ceased to be necessary *in its original form*, but what form should it then take? Miss
Baber, BCH's second Warden, writing in the Annual Report after her first full year in
office, was blunt; "The work becomes heavier and the standard of the work required
rises. **It is no longer possible to manage only with amateurs. We must have a nucleus
of paid trained workers.**" [3] Putting her words into bold type, Miss Baber knew she
would be ruffling feathers; there were those who distrusted 'professionalism' and
wanted to continue the work of BCH solely on the basis of high-minded altruism. But
Miss Baber had seen the future, and knew how it would work. Which is not to say that
she was dismissing the work of volunteers, rather recognizing that in the long run the
professionals would inevitably move to centre stage. Writing nearly twenty years earlier,
the future Prime Minister Clement Attlee (once a Toynbee Hall volunteer) had said:
A settlement must, it appears to me, move with the times, and those
that merely carry on the old work that was applicable to earlier days are
not being as useful as they might. A settlement today must be in closer
touch than ever with the best minds of the working people of the district.
It must be free from any taint of what is often described as charity-mongering
and of any idea of superiority. It would be well if it could be supported and
controlled by the people of the district, and get away entirely from the idea
that it was supported by charitably disposed persons from outside. [4]

The fact is that, in its early decades, the majority of the members of the BCH Council were not residents of Fulham, and it is only gradually, since World War Two, that local representation has grown. Similarly, it took a while before the possibility of involving men in both the direction and work of BCH was considered. A Special Meeting of the Executive Committee in 1932 was the first occasion when the question of inviting men to serve on the Council was considered, and the feeling was unanimously that it was a good idea. [5] Duly that year The Earl of Haddo, The Hon S. Lawrence, Prebendary Propert and J. E. Talbot were elected to Council. Getting men actually working at BCH (aside from various medical professionals) took a little longer. The topic first arose in 1941:

> The question of a man Club-leader, to live out, was considered.
> Regarding the possible employment of a Conscientious Objector,
> the Council agreed there was no objection in principle to their engaging
> one, but that in practice the difficulties might prove to be very great, and
> applications would have to be considered individually. [6]

However it was not until the war was over that the first male worker was taken on and the Appointments Committee noted, "It was generally felt that the time had come to appoint a male Club Leader, the present type of Club boy being better dealt with by men." [7] The ground-breaker was Gerald Howard-Smith, 23, a Harrovian, who had studied at the Law Society and at Sandhurst, before serving in France, Belgium and Holland, where he was wounded. Recovered, he was now a candidate for ordination, and was installed for three months, his salary of £3 per week being covered by the LCC Play Centre Grant.

The war also provoked thoughts on a higher plane about the whole nature of Settlement work and its place in the social landscape. Betraying what might seem a rather premature confidence in allied victory, the British Association of Residential Settlements (BARS) [8] circulated a memorandum for discussion in September 1941:

> PRESENT PROBLEMS, SETTLEMENT POLICY
> & POST-WAR RECONSTRUCTION.
> Residential Settlements during the war have been occupied with serving their
> neighbours in a large and diverse number of ways. Very few have been able
> to maintain a normal programme of recreational and educational activity.
> This swinging of the resources of Settlements to meet new wartime needs
> has had a number of effects:-
> 1. The breakdown of habits of work and ways of thought some of which
> were ripe for change.
> 2. The awakening of initiative and the rebirth of pioneering thought and action.
> 3. A greater emphasis on immediate personal help in many cases
> of a 'relief' character.
> 4. A closer link with the neighbourhood and the Local Authorities.
> 5. A concentration of thought and effort on the immediate present
> rather than long-time planning of constructive work.
> 6. A bolstering up of depleted finances by means of grants and
> gifts from sources which will not continue to be available." [9]

The memorandum went on to throw out questions across the whole spectrum of Settlement life: What is the function of a Settlement? Who ought to live in a Settlement? What constitutes a Settlement? By whom and how should a Settlement be governed? What kind of premises should a Settlement possess? How ought a Settlement to be financed? It further noted that already in 1941, a range of government planning had begun for reconstruction in the post-war world: a Ministry of Reconstruction under Arthur Greenwood had been established, Sir William Beveridge was looking into Social Services, the Board of Education had put out a discussion document, Political & Economic Planning Broadsheets were being issued every fortnight, quite revolutionary ideas were in common circulation to do with health provision and public ownership - what contribution could Settlements make, and where, in this maelstrom of potential change, would Settlements find a place, find a new role?

BCH took this all very seriously and a conference was convened on 1 October 1941 to go over all the questions raised. Miss Wickham opened by reviewing BCH history to date:

> Co-operation with local government has increased steadily, though the Settlement has to some extent always preserved a certain independence of thought such as was instanced by its disagreement with the Borough Council in earlier days over the question of housing … The History of the Settlement showed very clearly its adaptability to the changing and growing needs of the neighbourhood and its readiness always to come to the assistance of those who, even if they would, often could not help themselves. [10]

Mrs Stocks, Principal of Westfield College, spoke up for the 'amateur':

> It was sometimes stated that a statutory body could achieve much more than an individual. As against this, Octavia Hill herself admitted that she had felt lost when she surveyed the problem of Housing as a whole, but but was always restored when she returned to work in her few slum courts. Was it not because her roots went so deep, that the foundations she laid are bearing so great a structure today? And this raised the question of what was to be the driving force behind Social Service. Surely it should be 'Amateur Philanthropy' in its true meaning ('Amateur' - one who works for love: 'Philanthropy' - love of man) … Government departments were confined to the administration of laws, and some red tape was therefore inevitable. Amateur philanthropy is infinitely more free to have what might be called 'bias', directing and colouring its whole work. [10]

Miss Batten, Secretary of BARS, was rather more sanguine:

> Speaking on the Settlement of the Future, she gave it as her opinion that the day of Amateur Philanthropy was over, and that what was needed was a new educational policy for the Settlement movement … Settlements tend to cater for the easiest age-groups, e.g. young children and adolescents. Now the government is gradually taking over these age-groups, itself providing play centres and adolescent clubs, staffing them with well-trained and adequately paid staffs. Therefore Settlements should turn to the people for whom the government is not providing, e.g. adults. [10]

She was equally unvarnished in her view of the financing of Settlements:

> a. If government grants are accepted, then Settlements are being paid by the government to do its work, and criticism of government policy becomes difficult.
> b. At present too great reliance is placed on casual grants from Trust Funds (Pilgrim Trust, Save the Children Fund, etc), this is not sound financial policy.
> c. Voluntary subscriptions are, for obvious reasons, likely to diminish, and therefore

d. Settlements should become self-supporting, on the principle of "consumers' co-operation". To a much greater degree than at present, those who benefit by the Settlement's work should help to pay for it, and this would be much easier if the work was among adults. [10]

Finally, she said, every Settlement should be asking itself: is the nature and purpose of the Settlement understood by the people in the district? Is residence at the Settlement a *sine qua non*? Should residency be single-sex? Should the name 'Settlement' be changed?

In lobbing these grenades against the calm certainties of Settlement thinking to date, Miss Batten was starting a debate that continues to this day, and we can pick it up at regular intervals over the next six decades. Writing in the first post-war BCH Annual Report, Miss Emmie Dodds, the third Warden, commented:

Our traditional moral structure, based on Christianity, has been very largely rejected for a new morality founded on a false idea of "good citizenship" which is limited in its ideal to a love of one's neighbour ...

The government schemes prepared to provide social security have tended to be concerned with the preservation of the plan rather than the consolation of the individual. In this respect though it seems on the surface that the state is going to supply all those services hitherto provided by voluntary bodies - in fact it is preparing a more rigid structure which will produce a great number of misfits. So in our role as 'sappers' of the social services, we have to consider the results of these new influences and determine what we have to destroy and what we have to preserve in preparation for our new foundation. [11]

By 1954, as the worst of the post-war austerity began to lift, the fifth Warden, 'Dai' Wilson, was writing:

There are two things which all Settlements appear to have in common: a seeming inability to make ends meet and a deep sense of gratitude to those who, through their financial help, moral support and encouragement, enable them to pull the ends together ... we cannot afford any degree of 'preciousness' or separation from the world. Our life must be one of devotion and worship, but it must prepare us for and not separate us from 'secular activities.' We must keep in mind the necessity for leadership and Christian influence in wider spheres than our own domestic life ... It is not easy to see the shape which Settlement work will take during the next few years. We must be strong enough to adjust ourselves to new methods, courageous enough to stand by our beliefs and standards, and knowledgeable enough to be useful to those whose duty and calling lead them to positions of responsibility in the government of our city or nation. [12]

Change in these matters can sometimes seem to progress at geological speed, but by the sixties the debate had moved on. In 1962, the Council acknowledged, "It was not realistic to expect the same contribution from residents today as had been given in the past." [13] And again, in 1967, the Council gave extended time to the question:

There was considerable discussion on the purpose and practicability of Settlement residence. It was noted that most Settlements were now reducing the amount of residential accommodation. It was agreed that Council must continue to consider whether residence was a priority in Settlement work today. Points to be borne in mind were:-

1) The economic strain on Settlement funds of a small unit.
2) The quality of help given by residents to Settlement work

and to the neighbourhood.
3) The need for suitable accommodation in London,
especially for students and people from overseas.
4) The demands for accommodation received from the
neighbourhood which if met would occupy rooms now used as bedrooms. [14]

And the Council returned to the theme at even greater length, "which brought out different points of view," a couple of meetings later:

Most members thought that the individual contributions made by residents did not balance the expenditure of energy, time and thought, given by staff and that as pressures were increasing on staff serious consideration must be given to priorities … BCH was not providing hostel accommodation but invited people concerned with and interested in community life to join the staff as part of a team … To justify subsidised accommodation and fulfil the terms of our Constitution the contribution of a resident must enhance the life of the neighbourhood either by individual participation in Borough life or by supporting Settlement projects. [15]

By 1980, Judy Lister (the last Warden, the first Director) was minded to be blunt:
This year the Council of BCH and myself have been looking critically at the ways in which the Settlement is meeting its objectives. Often the traditions of an organisation tend to cloud judgement on how effective it is. Activities take place "because we've always done it." Now we cannot afford the luxury of activities for which we are not professionally or financially accountable … The movement towards self-help groups has of course been reflected in our fund-raising which becomes increasingly difficult as groups raise money for themselves and not for the Settlement as a whole. [16]

Her successor, Colin Barnes, reporting in September 1989, found himself in the middle of even more drastic changes in the way BCH received its monies:
There are a lot of indications that the nature of funding will change. We have known for some time that partnerships in funding for particular programmes of work are being advocated; such partnerships can involve local government, central government, trusts, charities and businesses. If you look at the list of our sources of income, you will see that we are already building those partnerships, as well as receiving significant individual contributions. There is also some discussion about service contracts whereby we would be invited to apply for monies to run specific services for specific groups. This is happening, I think, for two main reasons. One is that the demands on statutory provision are growing, and the big service providers are re-thinking whether they should, or can, do certain types of work. The other is that organisations like BCH can be more flexible, more responsive and more cost-effective than the statutory services. [17]

A year later BCH commissioned a CERT (Charities Effectiveness Review Trust) analysis. In amongst a good deal of management-speak, one thing emerged very clearly; if BCH had originally been dependent primarily on the goodwill of a number of high-minded and well-to-do supporters, it was now dependent primarily on the London Borough of Hammersmith & Fulham, which provided no less than 82% of the Settlement's annual income. Colin Barnes' successor, Barbara Backhaus, obviously knew where it was important to establish good relations:

Discussion with LBHF grants officers revealed that they are very pleased with the work done over the past year and with our ideas for future developments. They also stressed the need to draw up a service plan for next year and to set targets which can be measured, both in terms of level of service and 'outcome' i.e. the wider benefit of a service or activity. Most funders now require this kind of information and appropriate systems for monitoring progress, as well as some kind of long term or strategic plan. [18]

Reviewing the year in the 1988-89 Annual Report, Barbara Backhaus put it plainly: in a statement that may have had one or two of Mrs Creighton's original associates turning in their graves she said, "BCH is now firmly in the contract culture." [19]

In the context of this century-long shift from the pure Christian altruism of Mrs Creighton, Miss Wickham and their generation to the world of SWOT analyses (Strengths, Weaknesses, Opportunities, Threats), box-ticking and bottom-line budgeting, there is something symbolic in the report of a new worker, Eleanor O'Brien, at BCH in the mid-eighties:

My first task as Centre Worker at BCH was the opening of long-locked and ever-guarded cupboards which proved to be an experience never to be forgotten, exposing evidence of the Settlement's long-passed residential days. Excess household and bed linen was gratefully received by a number of voluntary organisations, including St Mungo's and Shelter. A large collection of odd plates was welcomed by a new Community Centre on the Bayonne Road Estate which had run out of funds for equipment. A wonderful collection of oddments went to Bradmore Kids Workshop for use by the children. The placing of an old tin bath tub of hand-made carbolic soap proved a little more difficult, but was, eventually, found a good home with one of the women's refuges. [20]

***

KEEPING IT UP

"Whatever the State does the voluntary societies will always be necessary. When the State takes over, there may not be the capacity, nor perhaps the inclination, to bother about the personal and spiritual side. That is a great mistake, however good the Welfare Service may be. At BCH we have been passing through a difficult time, and sometimes we have wondered if we would be able to carry on. But we must redouble our efforts because we simply cannot afford to let this kind of work go undone."

Dr J. W. C. Wand, Bishop of London [1]

One of the organisations with which BCH involved itself in its earliest years was Miss Arnould's Association for the Physically and Mentally Defective. Miss Arnould took on and 'worked miracles' with children excluded as hopeless from LCC special schools. Her methods were the basis on which much of today's Montessori system is founded. Miss Wickham recalled, "She had something like genius in training blind and crippled and defective people of all ages either to earn their living or to find happiness in developing their faculties." [2] This willingness to deal with people outside the regular categories, people with often deeply intractable difficulties, unresponsive, unrewarding to work with, people sometimes who have placed themselves outside the regular parameters of help, has been a hallmark of BCH activities throughout the hundred years of its existence. Writing long before the modern proliferation of the Welfare State, Clement Attlee signalled the special merit of voluntary work, "In all social work there is the great danger that must be avoided of treating people as cases, and grouping them in categories and statistical tables, so that one forgets that all the time one is dealing with individuals ... This danger is one to which official bodies and Government departments are prone: it is the function of the volunteer worker to correct it." [3]

For ten years, 1965 to 1975, BCH hosted the Prisoners' Wives Service. This had come into existence as an emergency service to bring aid to the wives of convicted men, and proved so valuable it was within a year given official accreditation to the Inner London Probation Service. Requests for visits to wives came mostly from Court Probation Officers, but also from Prison Welfare Officers, where a man had expressed worries about his family. Reporting on the first year's work, Sylvia Chancellor, who launched the idea, revealed a yawning need:

> Often we are the first person to see the wife and break the news of her husband's sentence. In the case of a first offender the wife usually has no idea where or how she can get assistance, and in nearly all cases the husband has left his family with outstanding debts. Our job at the first visit is to find out her financial liabilities, give her advice on where she can get help, give her information about prison visits, letters etc, but above all listen sympathetically to her personal worries ... The fact that we visit because we want to and not

as a representative of a public body is a great help in our relationship with the families. [4]

A couple of Annual Reports later, some examples were given of the situations the PWS visitors were encountering:

> Mrs C: she was the mother of a single, mentally retarded prisoner in a London prison. He did not come to the attention of the Welfare Officer until near his release date when he expressed concern about his mother who was seventy and living alone. A PWS visitor called immediately and found her living in acute poverty. She took what practical steps were possible to help and continued friendly visiting. No other welfare organisation was visiting the old lady.
>
> Mrs T: a Probation Officer at a court contacted the PWS after Mr T expressed concern that his wife did not turn up at court (Mr T was on remand in custody). Apparently, Mrs T was depressive, suicidal and had been ill. A PWS visitor went immediately. The home was in an almost derelict block of flats and the visitor could get no answer. Feeling uneasy she returned later the same evening and succeeded in getting admission to Mrs T's flat. Mrs T was not there but there was evidence of her having left hastily. The visitor made further enquiries and later found that Mrs T was indeed ill and in great need of help, both supportive and practical. [5]

A couple of years on and the work had multiplied:

> During the year we visited over 350 new families. At Christmas we were able to take presents to 212 families having a total of 450 children. The voluntary visitors either chose something they knew would be welcome or took money to the value of £1 for each wife and 50p for each child. This was made possible through the generosity of the Sheriffs' and Recorders' Fund, The National Association for the Care and Resettlement of Offenders, the Clothworkers Company and *The Evening News*. [6]

The PWS evidently answered a crying need and the only reason they left BCH after ten years was that they were offered free accommodation, phones and heating by the Probation and After Care Service.

BCH's other excursion into the field of prison-related work was a three year experiment funded by the Gulbenkian Foundation from April 1968 to April 1971. As the Senior Probation Officer at West London Magistrates Court, J. Claude Fubini, wrote in his introduction to the project:

> The voluntary after-care of persons who have undergone recent imprisonment and other institutional experience is by no means new. However, in the past, this has been on a limited scale and the greater amount of aid was given by the Discharged Prisoners Aid Societies ... [There is] the need of many ex-prisoners for simple encouragement and human understanding which can be given by sincere and warm-hearted volunteers with sound common sense and the ability to make themselves acceptable to those whom they seek to help ...
> A Home Office circular on this subject recognizes that "as a private individual, a volunteer may be able to establish a good relationship with an offender who would shun all contact with officials." [7]

Thus was launched the Hammersmith Voluntary After-Care Project, to be run by Winston Martin, formerly of the prison service, and later to become BCH's sixth Warden. Three years later, when the Gulbenkian grant ceased, the conclusions were positive, although it must have seemed that the Project had hardly begun to tackle the vastness of the problem:

> The part of the scheme which is unique and which we think could be usefully developed here or elsewhere is the group which has met regularly on Monday evenings… The discussion groups have been attended by probation officers, students, social workers, police, volunteers and accredited associates as well as by ex-prisoners and their families. The value was made obvious through the relaxed and frank exchanges and by the attitudes of the more successfully re-established ex-prisoners who gave active support to those newly released or less secure, especially in the vital ways - finding lodgings and a job. It has been encouraging to see the steady growth of feelings of responsibility and willingness to co-operate. [8]

> …

Another BCH initiative was LEAP (The Local Employment Advice Project), set up in April 1986, trying to explore new ways to work with long-term unemployed people on two estates in Fulham, Lancaster Court and Robert Owen. Gratifyingly, after a year it was reported that "the people using our facilities were people who had resisted initiatives in the past" and the LEAP workers could record some breakthrough, with people going on to training or into employment:

> Two women went on to do 'O' levels and one of them is going to take the CQSW and become a social worker. We encourage the women to develop their own skills, and found that many were skilled in needlecraft; we ran a sewing and mixed craft group; one woman is embarking on a full-time training course in craft design; another two have started their own business producing hand-knitted garments and making Black hair accessories. [9]

After two years of modest progress, it was decided to expand LEAP into the White City, recognised as the Borough's largest and most deprived estate, with the highest unemployment figures. There again the workers found that their clientele was mainly black single mothers, tied to the estate by having to care for their children, and, unlike other unemployed people, not therefore in a position so readily to move off the estate during the day to explore work possibilities. A successful application for funding support from the BBC, whose vast corporate headquarters sit right next to the White City estate, led to undreamt-of developments:

> The training course in office skills for White City residents proved to be very successful for getting people into employment with the BBC, and as a result we are running another course. LEAP's involvement here was in interviewing, selecting and supporting the participants and the outreach worker, ensuring that suitable jobs were found and that equal opportunities practice was observed throughout the whole process … The methods adopted by LEAP appear to be very effective and bring about progress and development for both groups and individuals. [10]

A year later however, the co-ordinator, Kristine Wellington, had to report that not all was well:

> As a result of the Council's poll tax capping, existing community workers are being redeployed, which means there will be no community workers at all to service this estate. I feel particularly angry about this because the black community, especially women with children, are the people most affected. [11]

LEAP kept going through various funding vicissitudes, and Kristine Wellington's reports maintained a determined optimism:

Our seventh year has been most exciting. We have exceeded the targets set by the Economic Development Unit and achieved and increased our grant at the start of the financial year. The work on White City estate and Edward Woods estate has taken off. Earlier this year we commenced the Paragon Employment Advice sessions. This has been achieved by a number of agencies working to provide a weekly one-stop service to local residents. Throughout 1992-93 enquiries from estate-based employment surgeries totalled 646.[12]

She went on to list flourishing computer courses with glowing thanks from successful graduates, the establishment of a resource and advice centre at BCH and of a Parent & Toddlers Group, but:

After all this, the Local Authority have earmarked LEAP for closure next year, due to their reduction in expenditure. LEAP would like to thank all the clients, users and service providers who have written letters to Councillors on our behalf.[12]

Somehow, LEAP struggled on for another year but:

Without core funding the work undertaken was limited ... Thanks to the provision of a crèche and a carefully targeted outreach strategy, women who would never otherwise have been able to take up the opportunity of training were recruited for the courses. Despite being unemployed for up to a decade, six of the eleven taking part found jobs within two months of completing the course and a seventh participant went on to take up further training.[13]

...

The groups most obviously marginalised by society, and whose needs BCH has perennially returned to, are the physically disabled and those with learning disabilities. Over the last fifty years BCH has hosted various clubs for these groups, which have had to grapple, not always successfully, with problems of transport and access. The latest and most imaginative scheme for learning disabled people began in June 1999 as a joint pilot project with Hammersmith and Fulham Action on Disability (HAFAD). After three months preparatory work, the Mentoring Project's co-ordinator, Sarah Duignan, gave a presentation to BCH trustees:

The project aims to match volunteer mentors with young disabled people, taking a broad definition of disability, so mentors may work with people with learning disabilities, mental health problems, physical disabilities and sensory impairments. Volunteers will work 1 to 1 with young people, supporting them in thinking about their goals in life and how to achieve them. This may include support around employment, training, housing, social activities, gaining confidence, improving self-esteem etc. It may also involve practical support such as helping preparation for interviews and filling in forms ...There would be a training programme for volunteers, safety issues being paramount because mentors and mentees would be meeting away from BCH ... She expected the first partnerships to be set up by Christmas [1999].[14]

The scheme was so obviously a good idea that there was a waiting list more or less from the outset. What began as an eighteen-month pilot had sustained for four years when the Director, Karen Osborn, reported to the Trustees:

The project is going really well. Recently nine new mentors were trained and are now being matched with young disabled people. There is still quite a waiting list for mentors ... Staff went to a National Mentoring Network event and were presented with a Certificate in Approved Provider Standard for Best Practice.[15]

118

However, and there has to be a however:
Identifying potential funders for the next financial year is proving difficult.
Many of the larger charitable funders recently changed their priorities: whereas
two or three years ago, young and disabled people were in favour, now there
seems to be a move towards funding mental health, drugs, homelessness,
domestic violence and community development - all 'un-sexy' areas which
have missed out over the last ten years. And, as usual, funders are very reluctant
to fund things which aren't new. This means we have had to try and completely
re-package the project as something new. [15]

BCH

June 1999: a Mentoring partnership at work.

Somehow the funding was sustained, and in 2002 a parallel project, Workwise, came on stream. At the same time an offshoot of the Mentoring Project saw the setting up of Peer Support and Peer Mentoring where, as a further part of building up these youngsters' self-esteem, they monitored and mentored each other. In 2004 the Annual Report was upbeat about both fields:

Workwise supports young people with learning disabilities to access and succeed in training and employment. We provide one-to-one help from starting to think about a career, to assessing learning and training, to work experience, volunteering, writing CVs, doing job searches and going to interview ...

The core work of the Mentoring Project is recruiting, training and supporting volunteers to mentor young people with learning disabilities. In the last year we have supported 27 young people with the help of 24 mentors. We have used innovative ways of engaging and supporting young people through peer mentoring and facilitating peer support networks. We've carried out educational work and piloted a really exciting Creative Mentoring programme, where young people work with artists to develop new skills. [16]

According to the 2006 Annual Report only 17% of people with learning disabilities are in paid work, and BCH wants to change that, at least in the London Borough of Hammersmith & Fulham. The testimony of two young beneficiaries is eloquent: "Workwise helps me find good places to work and helped me think about my future ... I think Workwise is very good for supporting people." "Having a mentor was good because with their help, I was able to go out more and experience new things. I would have been too nervous to go on my own." [17]

...

Dropping in to BCH, there is always something going on, as the current diary shows (see p 130); some of the events belong to BCH, such as the 'Busy Bees' and the Art Club, but many are run by organisations who pay rent and who find in BCH a sympathetic milieu - Weight Watchers, Alcoholics Anonymous, the Bangladeshi, Sudanese and Iraqi Associations and Sahaja Yoga for example, and then there are the politicians who find 378 Lillie Road a convenient place for surgeries. This first impression is the public face of BCH, but go over to the far corner of reception and pick up one of the several flyers displayed for your interest and you see what BCH does in its hundredth year - much of it off the premises, often in the homes of the people it is serving.

These programmes can be traced back to January 1981, when a scheme called Keep Warm was launched with backing from the Manpower Services Commission, funds committed under their Community Enterprise Programme until March 1984. The idea was simultaneously to tackle two pressing national problems; high fuel prices and high unemployment. The scheme provided low-cost insulation, draught-proofing and a heating advice service to the elderly, the disabled, or others on low income to ensure they used the fuel they were paying for as efficiently as possible. At the same time, the staff who were employed doing this work were being taken off the unemployed register if they had been on it for over six months (aged 18 to 25) or over twelve months (aged over 25). The service found an immediate market and at the end of its first year had employed 24 people and given service to 600 households in the Borough. But, wrote Judy Lister:

120

The government has prematurely terminated the Community Enterprise Programme and a new Community Programme is to begin on 1 October 1982. The Community Programme involves larger numbers of staff, the majority on a part-time basis and with a lower weekly wage. It will be impossible in practical terms for Keep Warm to operate under the new programme. The Management Committee will be pursuing alternative sources of funding for 1983/4 to save the project from closure ... There is little encouragement for organisations like BCH to embark on new projects when the government prematurely closes a successful programme and then expects us to co-operate in delivering a new programme mid-stream. Over 90% of CEP projects in London are sponsored by voluntary organisations but this time the new scheme, for BCH at least, represents an unacceptable compromise at the expense of the long-term unemployed. [18]

The need for the service offered by Keep Warm could hardly have been plainer; in an article in the *Guardian* on 20 January 1982, a potential customer was quoted as saying, "In the past few weeks, during the severe weather, the choice has been between heating and eating, so I ended up not paying any rent." Happily further funding was secured from the Borough and from the GLC to sustain the work till 1985. Successive Annual Reports cited 466, 504, 400 and 757 jobs completed. The staff however recognized that, valuable and worthwhile though the scheme was, funding could always go away and thoughts began to turn:

[although] there seems no reason to regard the project as being of a temporary nature, nevertheless innovation is required and hopefully the project can in the future become involved in complementary work such as security in the home for the elderly in the Borough, where the same client group will be involved. Equally, involvement of the project in assisting the Council's Social Services Department in installing aids for handicapped people may prove to be an area of co-operation in the future. [19]

The thought about security in the home was picked up promptly and Keep Safe was born in January 1985. After four years work, over 5,000 residents had had security equipment installed in their homes and the waiting list continued to grow. At the same time, the Keep Warm team were refining their thinking as to how to expand what they offered:

On a day-to-day basis, during the course of our home visits and when talking to our clients, we are in a perfect position to see first-hand gaps in the services offered by both statutory and voluntary agencies in the Borough. Some of these needs are simple and could be met with minimal funding and contained within present resources, i.e. a Small Jobs Scheme: we are all aware of how difficult it is to have a curtain rail fixed or repaired, a shelf put in place or a simple decorating job undertaken; if you are elderly, disabled or housebound, the lack of such a facility can cause distress and worry and diminish the quality of life. [20]

The Small Jobs Scheme was duly incorporated into the Keep Warm work flow, and KW received another boost when they successfully contracted their services to the Royal Borough of Kensington & Chelsea, which was just as well because:

As we enter our tenth year, we will be facing what seems to be an insurmountable obstacle of a 56% cut in funding which is proposed by the Council. Though we have been flexible and imaginative in our responses to past changes in Borough politics and funding, we are

(with many other community organisations) appalled at what seems to be an end to community care as we know it. [21]
By 1993 Keep Warm was calling itself Keep Warm/Care & Repair, with the new addition being "an independent home improvement agency that provides help to organise small or large works for the elderly and/or disabled." The thrust as ever being to give vulnerable residents the confidence and support to stay in their own homes in reasonable comfort and without worries about maintenance. Keep Warm could by now boast over 10,000 jobs of insulation completed since its inception in 1981, and, still with a waiting list, it seems amazing that there could be any question of shutting it down. BCH instanced a not untypical example of the kind of household they had dealt with:

> Mr and Mrs T are lifelong residents of Fulham. He is 79 years old, she is 81. Mr T suffers from dementia and Mrs T has pernicious anaemia. Mrs T applied to Keep Warm for draughtproofing work to their rented home. When visited by Keep Warm staff to assess the work, it was noted that the only heating was electric bar fires, and the house was very cold. Mrs T explained that they were frightened by fuel bills and could not have the fires on for any period of time. Their plight was referred to Care & Repair who then arranged a home visit. Mr and Mrs T were counselled about fuel debt and energy savings. Their problems were further compounded by only having an outside toilet. We applied for a grant to have central heating installed, which is now in place. We successfully applied to a local charity for financial help to clear a long standing fuel debt and a contribution towards their winter quarter's fuel bills in the future. We have also successfully gained grant aid to install a lavatory at ground floor level inside. This work is currently in progress. We referred them to Keep Safe who will carry out security work in their home in the near future. In a relatively short time we have greatly improved the warmth, comfort and security of the couple's home and thereby the quality of their lives. [22]

Today the Small Jobs Scheme, the Home Safety Check Scheme, the Keep Safe Scheme and the Care & Repair Scheme (which incorporates the distribution of Homeline alarms) are the descendants of those admirable initiatives of the 1980s. While many of the schemes are aimed at the elderly, disabled, housebound, and those on low incomes, there is one other service targeting the opposite end of the age spectrum; CARES (Children's Accident Reduction Education + Support) which offers safety advice as well as installing stair gates, smoke alarms, door jammers, plug covers and the like to families with young children.

Another BCH project started as Careline, has been through various name-changes, accompanied by subtle changes in the work-description, and is now called Homeline. Its origins may traced back to something called Health in Retirement, which turned into the Well Pensioner Project. It was described by its co-ordinator, Polly Clark, as follows...

> Three main areas of work with elderly people in the Borough:
> 1) Phone out Careline to ease the isolation of elderly housebound residents, operated by volunteers aged 50+.
> 2) One to one counselling offered to the 50+ age group in their homes or in BCH, by volunteer counsellors, themselves aged 50+.
> 3) Groups, classes and sessions on a variety of health-related topics in BCH and other locations in the Borough.

Over the past year, 11 volunteers made approximately 6250 phone calls to an average of 25 clients, Monday to Friday for fifty weeks of the year. Counselling: In the year, 20 volunteers each undertook a total of 45 hours training, and 50 hours of supervision. 58 clients referred for counselling received a total of 190 sessions of one to one counselling. With the clients I see that is a total of about 310 sessions. Classes, course and talks: about 30 over the year. [23]

That was 1993, by 1994 all that survived was the Careline phoning, with a contract from the Borough Social Services to call 40 isolated elderly people every day. It was established that if there was no reply three days in a row, Social Services or a named relative would be contacted. The number called was over fifty a further year on, and inevitably there was a waiting list. Careline added another refinement in 1996, for those who were up to it and wanted it; the Walking Project offered an arm to lean on for those who might have lost confidence about going outdoors on their own. Careline further expanded its portfolio the next year; adding home visits and hospital visits, it now had 74 clients of whom 47 were over eighty. It also sent out 129 birthday/get well/Christmas cards. The testimonials were gratifying: 'My friends at Careline remember my birthday when no-one else does', 'Careline stopped me from killing myself after my husband died', 'Careline is my friend.' The service, now called Homeline, continues, the demand unabated.

One further service is well worth a mention; begun in 2001 in collaboration with Charing Cross Hospital, Home From Hospital plainly filled a need:

Courtesy Stan James *The Gazette*

April 2003: BCH volunteer Gladys Barcelo
gives 89 year old Phyllis Bowman a manicure.
Discharged from Charing Cross Hospital, Phyllis was paired with Gladys
under the Home from Hospital scheme. "She's marvellous," they both say.

The scheme was introduced in the Annual Report for 2001-2002:

> After a long hospital stay - in a warm safe place where there are lots of people and everything is provided - it can be a shock to return home alone. People can be isolated, depressed and scared. This scheme supports older people through hospital discharge and helps them settle in again at home. The friendship and support of volunteers helps patients to regain confidence and independence, improving the quality of life and - we hope - reducing re-admissions.[24]

...

The last time BCH worked out the sums, in 2003, they calculated that over seventy volunteers had given the Settlement 13,000 hours of their time that year. No such calculations were done in earlier years but it is safe to say the volume of effort has not slackened in the Settlement's first hundred years, and BCH is firm in its intention of maintaining its contribution to the community for another hundred years. The words of Clement Attlee, speaking at a reception in his honour at Toynbee Hall in 1947, remain true today:

> Britain has a tradition of voluntary effort that is not confined to any one class of the community. Alongside everything done by the local authority and by the state there are people who want to do a bit more ... This country will never become a people of an exclusive and omnipotent state ... I believe that we shall always have, alongside the great range of public services, the voluntary services which humanize our national life and bring it down from the general to the particular. We must keep stretching out to new horizons.[25]

***

BCH CHAIRMEN & WARDENS/DIRECTORS

Chairmen

Mrs Louise Creighton	1908-1932
Mrs Sarah Bailey	1932-1936
Lady Gwen Moberly	1936-1947
Lady Doris Blacker (Acting)	1947-1948
Lady Portia Bland	1948-1952
Mrs Eveleen Fisher-Rowe	1952-1955
Lady Doris Blacker	1955-1959
Miss Phyllis Brooks	1959-1972
The Rev R. E. J. Dawson	1972-1977
Royden Morgan	1977-1996
Mrs Maya Donelan	1997-

Wardens

Catherine Wickham*	1908-1935
Sybil Baber	1935-1942
Emmie Dodds	1942-1946
Kathleen Worster	1946-1953
Daisy 'Dai' Wilson**	1953-1971
Winston Martin	1971-1975
Rodney Moore	1975-1978

Directors

Judy Lister	1979-1984
Colin Barnes	1985-1994
Barbara Backhaus	1994-1999
Karen Osborn	1999-2007

Chief Executive

Rory Gillert	2007-

* Made a Freeman of the Metropolitan Borough of Fulham 1935
** Made a Freeman of the London Borough of Hammersmith 1973

BCH Diaries in former years...

MONDAY.

12. 0 noon— 2. 0 p.m.	Invalid Kitchen (every day).
2. 0 p.m.— 4. 0 p.m.	Clinic : Gas Session.
5.15 p.m.— 6.45 p.m.	Play Guild.
8. 0 p.m.—10.30 p.m.	Senior Mixed Club.

TUESDAY.

9. 0 a.m.— 11.30 a.m.	Clinic: Vision Session.
2. 0 p.m.— 4. 0 p.m.	Infant Massage Clinic.
2. 0 p.m.— 3.30 p.m.	Clinic; Minor Ailments, Doctor's Session.
	Teaching Children in Hospital.
6. 0 p.m.— 7.15 p.m.	Junior Boys' Club.
	Remedial Exercises.
	Women's Holiday Interviews.
8. 0 p.m.—10. 0 p.m.	Women's Folk Dancing Class.
	Intermediate Girls' Club.

WEDNESDAY.

10. 0 a.m.—11. 0 a.m.	Clinic: Minor Ailments, Doctor's Session.
2. 0 p.m.— 4. 0 p.m.	Clinic: Gas Session.
2.30 p.m. 4.30 p.m.	Child Guidance Clinic.
	Women's Fellowship.
2. 0 p.m.—10. 0 p.m.	Foot Clinic.
5.15 p.m.— 6.45 p.m.	Play Guild.
5.15 p.m.— 6.15 p.m.	Child Guidance Conference.
7.30 p.m.— 9. 0 p.m.	School Leavers' Club.
8.30 p.m.—10. 0 p.m.	Senior Girls' "Keep Fit" Class.
	Senior Boys' "Keep Fit" Class.
	Religious Drama Class.

THURSDAY.

10. 0 a.m.—12. 0 noon	C.C.H.F. Assessment Committee.
2. 0 p.m.— 4. 0 p.m.	Infant Massage Clinic.
3. 0 p.m.— 4. 0 p.m.	Women's "Keep Fit" Class.
5.15 p.m.— 6.45 p.m.	Play Guild.
8. 0 p.m.—10. 0 p.m.	Rangers and Scouts.
	Senior Lecture and Dance Evening.
	Workers' Educational Association Class.

FRIDAY.

10. 0 a.m.—11.30 a.m.	Clinic: Minor Ailments, Doctor's Session.
2.30 p.m.— 4.30 p.m.	Child Guidance Clinic.
2. 0 p.m.— 4. 0 p.m.	Teaching Children in Hospital.
2. 0 p.m.— 3.30 p.m	Nutrition Clinic.
5.15 p.m.— 6.45 p.m.	Play Guild.
8. 0 p.m.—10. 0 p.m	Senior Boys' Ping Pong Club.
8.30 p.m.—10.30 p.m	Senior Dramatic Class.

SATURDAY AND SUNDAY.

Occasional Dances (Saturdays).   Discussions (Sundays).

1938

ACTIVITIES.

DAILY.—Play Centre; Child Guidance.

MONDAY.—Intermediate Club; Junior Girls' Club; Youth Club; Adult Club.

TUESDAY.—Old People's Club; Junior Boys' Club; Youth Club; Women's Country Holiday Fund.

WEDNESDAY.—Women's Fellowship; Junior Girls' Club; Intermediate Club; Adult Club.

THURSDAY.—Junior Boys' Club; 1st Thursday in month Social Workers' Lunch Club; Youth Club; Adult Club.

FRIDAY.—Old People's Club; Wolf Cubs; Youth Club; Adult Club.

SATURDAY.—Junior Football; Senior Football; Cricket; Cycling; Dances; Week-end Camps in summer for club members.

Care Committee Work for Queensmill, Everington Street, Beaufort House and Star Road Schools.

Children's Country Holiday Fund.

Old People's Welfare.

1948

Monday	Blind Club	2–4 p.m.
	Wives Club	8 p.m. twice monthly
Tuesday	Western Chapter Meeting	10.45 a.m. (monthly)
	Social Workers' Lunch	12.45 p.m. (monthly)
	Chiropody Clinic	10.30 to 5 p.m.
	Pensioners' Clubs	2 to 4 p.m.
	Women's Holiday Fund	2.30 p.m.
	Toc H	8 p.m.
Wednesday	Women's Fellowship	2.30–4 p.m.
	Hospital Club	2 p.m.–3.30 p.m.
	Overseas Social Centre	8 p.m.–10.30 p.m.
Thursday	Marriage Guidance Council	10 a.m. to 1 p.m. and 7.30 to 9.30 p.m.
	Blind Club	2–4 p.m.
	Wives' Club	2.30–4 p.m.
	Old Tyme Dancing	8 p.m.–10 p.m.
Friday	Pensioners' Club	2–4 p.m.
	Pensioners' Club at West Kensington	2–4 p.m.
	Whist Drive	7.30 p.m.
Saturday	Club for the Physically Handicapped	3 p.m.–6 p.m. (monthly)
	Overseas Social Centre	Dances (occasional)

1958

ACTIVITIES 1967/68

Monday

Pre School Play Group	9.30 am—12.30 pm
Under Fives Trolley Time	1 pm—4 pm
Hospital Club	1.45 pm—3.15 pm
Blind Club	1.30 pm—3.30 pm
Marriage Guidance	5.30 pm—8.30 pm
Women's Club	8 pm fortnightly
Amalgamated Ass. of Woodworkers	7.30 pm fortnightly
Chiropody Clinic	1 pm—6.30 pm

Tuesday

Pre School Play Group	9.30 am—12.30 pm
Under Fives Trolley Time	9.30 am—12 noon
Social Workers' Lunch	1 pm—4 pm monthly
Chiropody Clinic	12.45 pm
Pensioners' Clubs	2 pm—4 pm
Crafts Class	2 pm—4 pm
Women's Holiday Fund	2.30 pm
'The Open Door Club'	7.30 pm—9.30 pm
Toc H. (Men)	8 pm—10 pm

Wednesday

Pre School Play Group	9.30 am—12.30 pm
Chiropody Clinic	9.30 am—12 noon
Under Fives Trolley Time	1 pm—4 pm
Women's Fellowship	2.30 pm—4 pm
Overseas Social Centre	7.30 pm—10.30 pm
Mo-peds Band	8 pm—10.30 pm

Thursday

Pre School Play Group	9.30 am—12.30 pm
Chiropody Clinic	9.30 am—12 noon
Under Fives Trolley Time	1 pm—4 pm
Blind Club	1.30 pm—3.30 pm
Old Time Dancing	8 pm—10 pm
Steel Band	8 pm—10.30 pm

Friday

Pre School Play Group	9.30 am—12.30 pm
Under Fives Trolley Time	1 pm—4 pm
Pensioners' Club at West Kensington	2 pm—4 pm
Whist Drive	7.30 pm
Toc. H. (Women)	8 pm—10 pm

Saturday

Club for the Physically Handicapped	3 pm—6 pm monthly
Overseas Social Centre	Dances—occasional

1968

128

Agoraphobic & Friends Self Help Group	7.30 pm Monday
Amalgamated Association of Woodworkers (U.C.A.T.T)	7.30 pm alternate Mondays
Blind Club	1.30 - 3.30 pm Monday
Chiropody	Monday pm, all day Wednesday, Thursday pm.
Creche	1.45 - 3.15 pm Thursday
Craft Class	2.00 - 4.00 pm Tuesday
English for Immigrants	10.00 - 12.noon Tuesday & Thursday
Folk Art	10.00 - 12 noon Thursday
Food Co-op	Tuesday, Wednesday, Friday, 1.30 - 2.00 pm
Fulham & District Branch of the British Diabetic Association	Second Thursday of the month at 8 pm.
Fulham Social & Recreational Club	8.00 - 10.00 pm Friday
Gujarati	5.45 - 7.45 pm Tuesdays
Literacy Tutorials	7.00 - 9.00 pm Monday
Marriage Guidance	By appointment
Open Door Club	7.00 pm Tuesday
Physically Handicapped Club	2.00 - 5.00 pm First Saturday in month
Playgroup	10.00 - 12.00 noon Daily
Senior Citizen's Day Centre	10.00 am - 4.00 pm Tuesday & Friday
Scout Test Class	7.30 pm Wednesday
Single Parents in Fulham (SPIF)	1.45 - 3.15 pm Thursday
Social Workers Luncheon Club	Second Wednesday of month at 12.30
Toc H	8.00 - 10.00 pm Tuesday & Friday
West London OAP's & Trade Union Joint Action Branch	Fourth Saturday in month at 3.00 pm.
Women's Club	7.30 pm alternate Mondays
Women's Fellowship	1.30 - 3.30 pm Wednesday
Women's Group	By appointment
Work Group	10.30 am - 1.00 pm Daily
Yoga	1.45 - 3.15 pm Thursday

1978

129

Club/Group	Time	Contact
MONDAY		
MP's Surgery	9am – 11am	Greg Hands Office 020 7835 5446
Art Club	11am – 1.30pm	Stuart Moon
Parents in Recovery (AA)	11 am – 1pm	Stuart Moon
NA	1:30pm – 3pm	Stuart Moon
Womens Club (Alternate weeks)	8pm – 10pm	Stuart Moon
TUESDAY		
Weight Watchers	11am – 1:30pm	Tel : 08457 123 000
Busy Bees	12pm – 3:30pm	Stuart Moon
OOT	4:30pm – 10pm	Stuart Moon
AA	7pm – 9pm	Stuart Moon
Sahaja Yoga	7pm – 9pm	Stuart Moon
WEDNESDAY		
Craft Group	2pm – 4pm	Brenda Griffiths Tel : 020 7736 0864
Fulham Academy	5pm – 7pm	
OOT	6pm – 9pm	Stuart Moon
Life Drawing	7pm – 9pm	Angela Mackay Tel : 020 7386 9210

We make every effort to ensure that groups are accessible to everyone. If you are a community or self help group and wish to hire a room, or for any other information contact Stuart Moon on 020 7385 9689 smoon@creightonhouse.org

Club/Group	Time	Contact
THURSDAY		
Older Womens Health Group	10am – 12:30pm	Stuart Moon
Bridge Group	12:30pm – 4:30pm	Stuart Moon
NA	12:00pm – 2:00pm	Stuart Moon
OOT	5:30pm – 10pm	Stuart Moon
AA	8pm – 9pm	Stuart Moon
Weight Watchers	6:30pm – 8:30pm	08457 123 000
FRIDAY		
Friday Club (Alternate weeks)	1:30pm – 3:30pm	Stuart Moon
Kixa Self-Defence	7:30pm – 9:30pm	
AA	8pm – 9pm	Stuart Moon
SATURDAY		
Conservative Councillor Surgery	9:30am – 10:30am	
Bangladeshi Welfare Association	11am – 1pm	
Iraqi Association	4:30pm – 6:30pm	
SUNDAY		
AA	10am – 1pm	Stuart Moon
Rainbow Club	3pm – 4pm	Mrs Jenkins Tel : 020 8894 5270
Sudanese Development Association	1pm – 4pm	
Mount Carmel	6pm – 9pm	Mrs Jones Tel : 020 7731 6020
Spiritist Psychology Society	5:30pm – 9:30pm	Stuart Moon

Spring 2008

NOTES pp 1-11
CHAPTER ONE - FIRST SETTLERS
1.   *Letters and Other Writings of the late Edward Denison,*
                edited by Sir Baldwyn Leighton, Richard Bentley and Son, 1872, p 36.
2.   *Stray Studies,* J. R. Green, Macmillan, 1903, p 13.
3.   *Denison Letters,* op cit, p 8.
4.   Ibid, p 37.
5.   *Jacob's Answer to Esau's Cry,* Brooke Lambert,
                Contemporary Review, Volume 46, September 1884, p 377.
6.   *Denison Letters,* op cit, pp 227-228.
7.   *Helping the Poor,* Robert Whelan, Civitas, 2001, p 25.
8.   *The Social Worker,* Clement Attlee, G. Bell & Sons, 1920, pp 65-66.
9.   Green, op cit, p 129.
10.   *A Basketful of Memories,* Thomas Okey, Dent, 1930, p 56. Okey is one of the
        more remarkable examples of what Settlements can do for you; son of a
        Whitechapel basket-maker, he was apprenticed to his father's trade, but
        discovered through Toynbee Hall a facility for languages, which he worked at so
        assiduously that he ended up as the Serena Professor of Italian Studies at Cambridge
        University.
11.   *The Life of Frederick Denison Maurice,* edited by F. Maurice, 3rd Edition,
                2 Volumes, 1884, 2: 35.
12.   *Canon Barnett - His Life, Work, and Friends,* Henrietta Barnett,
                2 Volumes, John Murray, 1918, 2:265-6.
13.   *My Apprenticeship,* Beatrice Webb, Longmans Green, 1926, p 207.
14.   *Canon Barnett,* op cit, 2:193.
15.   *The Bitter Cry of Outcast London,* Andrew Mearns,
                edited by Anthony S. Wohl, reprinted by Leicester University Press, 1970.
16.   *Changes and Chances,* Henry Nevinson, Nisbet, 1923, pp 87-91.
17.   Okey, op cit, pp 50-51.
18.   *Power and Influence,* William Beveridge, Hodder & Stoughton, 1953, p 21.
19.   *Toynbee Hall - The First Hundred Years,* Asa Briggs & Anne Macartney,
                Routledge & Kegan Paul, 1984, p 62.
20.   *East London,* Walter Besant, 4th Edition, Chatto & Windus, 1903, pp 311-12.
21.   *Denison Letters,* op cit, pp 40-1.
22.   *Toynbee Record,* April 1892.
23.   *Life & Letters of Mandell Creighton,* Louise Creighton,
                2 Volumes, Longmans Green, 1904, 2:74.
24.   Ibid, 2:224.
CHAPTER TWO - THE CREIGHTONS
1.   *My Apprenticeship,* Beatrice Webb, Longmans Green, 1926, p 350.
2.   *Life & Letters of Mandell Creighton,* Louise Creighton,
                2 Volumes, Longmans Green, 1904, 1:398.
3.   Ibid, 1:399.
4.   Ibid, 1:50-51.
5.   Ibid, 1:75.
6.   Ibid, 1:141.
7.   *Blackwell Dictionary of Historians,* Blackwell Reference, 1988.
        The entry on Mandell Creighton was written by Peter Slee of the University of
        Durham, who concludes "Creighton's insistence that history was not a 'moral
        science' and that its aim was 'to give off light without heat' is his greatest
        contribution to the growth of historical scholarship in Britain."

8.   *Portraits & Sketches*, Edmund Gosse, Heinemann, 1912, pp 178-9.
9.   *Memoir of a Victorian Woman: Reflections of Louise Creighton*
                    edited by James Covert, Indiana University Press, 1994, pp 63-4.
10.   *Creighton Life & Letters*, op cit, 1:226.
11.   Ibid, 1:368.
12.   Ibid, 1:372.
13.   *University and Other Sermons*, Mandell Creighton,
                    edited by Louise Creighton, Longmans Green, 1903, pp 179-80, 183-4.
14.   *Creighton Life & Letters*, op cit, 1:256.
15.   Ibid, 1:392.
16.   *Louise Creighton Memoir*, op cit, p 86.
17.   Ibid, p 90.
18.   *Creighton Life & Letters*, op cit, 1:398-9.
19.   *Louise Creighton Memoir*, op cit, p 112.
20.   Ibid, p 113.
21.   *The Letters of Queen Victoria*, Third Series, Volume III, John Murray, 1932, p 96.
22.   *Creighton Life & Letters*, op cit, 2:220.
23.   *Portraits in Miniature*, Lytton Strachey, Chatto & Windus, 1931, p 216.
24.   *Creighton Life & Letters*, op cit, 2:260.
25.   Gosse, op cit, p 190.
26.   *A Victorian Marriage - Mandell and Louise Creighton*,
                    James Covert, Hambledon and London, 2000, pp 255-6.
27.   *Our Partnership*, Beatrice Webb, Longmans Green, 1948, pp 135-6.
28.   *The Women's Movement in the Church of England 1850-1930*,
                    Brian Heeney, Oxford, 1988, pp 98-99.
29.   *Our Partnership*, op cit, p 206.
30.   Strachey, op cit, p 214.
31.   Gosse, op cit, pp 195-6.
32.   Lambeth Palace Archives, letter of 28 January 1906, 3678/85.
33.   The publications, all edited by Louise, all published by Longmans Green, are, in
                    order of appearance...
                    The Church and The Nation: Charges and Addresses, 1901.
                    Historical Essays and Reviews, 1902.
                    Thoughts on Education: Speeches and Sermons, 1902.
                    University and Other Sermons, 1903.
                    Historical Lectures and Addresses, 1903.
                    The Mind of St Peter and Other Sermons, 1904.
                    The Claims of the Common Life:
                    Sermons Preached in Merton College Chapel 1871-1874, 1905.
                    Counsels for the Young: Extracts from the Letters of Mandell Creighton, 1905.
34.   *Randall Davidson*, G. K. A. Bell, 2 Volumes, Oxford, 1935, 1:359.
35.   *Louise Creighton Memoir*, op cit, p 146.
36.   Heeney, op cit, p 93.
37.   Lambeth Palace Archives, letter of 10 November 1907, 3678/106.
38.   - - - , letter of 15 March 1908, 3678/108.
39.   - - - , letter of 7 May 1908, 3678/109.

CHAPTER THREE - "A PLAN THAT I HAVE IN MY HEAD..."

1.   *Life & Letters of Mandell Creighton*, Louise Creighton,
                    2 Volumes, Longmans Green, 1904, 1:323.

NOTES pp 21-30

2.   LH, DD/531, Box 3 [BCH3/3/1]. Note: Most of the records of Bishop Creighton
       House are held by Hammersmith & Fulham Archives and Local History Centre, at
       The Lilla Huset, 191 Talgarth Road, W6 8BJ. The collection was received as two
       accessions, DD/531 and DD/748, the former comprising twenty-one boxes, the latter
       seven. Some of the material was sorted on behalf of BCH by a freelance archivist,
       Daniel Capron, in 2001 and individual documents like this letter given reference
       numbers by him, but the bulk remains uncatalogued. Several more boxes of
       material, found in the course of preparing this history, will be transferred to the
       Archives this year, and given an accession reference number. In my footnotes, I
       designate all material *already* at the Lilla Huset at the time of this writing with the
       prefix LH.
3.   Interview, 24 January 2008.
4.   LH, DD/531, Box 1 [BCH1/66, p 5].
5.   LH, DD/531, Box 3 [BCH3/1/1].
6.   Lambeth Palace Archives, Davidson 141, ff 168-171.
7.   LH, DD/531, Box 1 [BCH1/1, p 3].
8.   *The Nineteenth Century*, Volume LXIII, March 1908, pp 365-380.
       The Rev[d] Richard Free should not be dismissed out of hand; he had
       voluntarily 'slummed' on the Isle of Dogs and written a classic account
       of the experience, *Seven Years Hard*. He did however think hunger-striking
       suffragettes should be left to die, and he was still railing against the
       appalling shortness of fashionable skirts in the mid-1920s.
9.   *The Nineteenth Century*, Volume LXIII, April 1908, pp 607-613.

CHAPTER FOUR - "THE VERGE OF CIVILISATION"

1.   *Life and Labour of the People in London*, Charles Booth,
                          Third Series, Volume Three, Macmillan, 1902, p 171.
2.   Miss Wickham is here quoting from *Fulham Old and New*,
       Charles James Fèret, 3 Volumes, The Leadenhall Press, 1900, 1:24.
       The Story of Bishop Creighton House, by C. M. L. Wickham and F. E. Hansford,
       revised, expanded, and re-published by the Fulham History Society in 1965.
       Though Miss Wickham's history is a pleasure to read and contains some anecdotes
       which are justly repeated in these pages, a cautious approach should
       be taken when she mentions dates; she obviously wrote from memory
       rather than checking her diary and says, for example, that BCH's opening was
       on 28 May 1908. Another short history, *Bishop Creighton House 1908-1985*, was
       subsequently put together by Humphrey Arthure, and I acknowledge a debt to both.
3.   *The Diary of Virginia Woolf 1915-1919*,
       Edited by Anne Olivier Bell, Hogarth Press, 1977, entry for 15 February 1919.
       The full entry is "...the verge of civilisation, on the outskirts of Fulham."
4.   Lambeth Palace Archives, FP Creighton 2.
5.   BCH 'Constitution' Folder.
                          Miss Harry to Messrs Pollard, Cooper & Thorowgood, 18 March 1943.
6.   Booth, op cit, pp 168, 173.
7.   Ibid, pp 169-70.
8.   Ibid, pp 170-71.
9.   Ibid, pp 171-72.
10.   Ibid, p 172.
11.   Ibid, p 174.
12.   LH, DD/531, Box 1 [BCH1/5, p 8].

13.   Quoted in *Helping the Poor*, Robert Whelan, Civitas, 2001, pp 164-65.
This book also has detailed case histories of several individual families who were assisted by the Fulham Office of the COS.

CHAPTER FIVE - "WORK WAS AT ONCE BEGUN"

1.   A regular watchword of Canon Barnett's, he had it on his wall at Toynbee Hall, this phrase is inscribed on his memorial tablet in Westminster Abbey.

2.   LH, DD/531, Box 1 [BCH1/1 p 5].

3.   LH, DD/531, Box 1 [BCH1/3 pp 3-4].

4.   This man is worth a digression: His full name was Henry Aldridge, Baron Bliss and Baron Barreto (a Portuguese title), who had inherited substantial estates from his uncle. He was to spend the last six years of his life cruising the Caribbean on his yacht, and died on board 9 March 1926, at anchor off Belize. He left his considerable fortune for good works in Belize, and to this day they celebrate the anniversary of his death as Baron Barreto Day.

5.   LH, DD/531, Box 1 [BCH2/1/3].

6.   BCH Council Minutes February 1951-November 1962. Also note that the Annual Report mentions 'two serious floods in the summer of 1954,' though Council Minutes only detail the one in May.

7.   *The Buildings of England, London 4: North*,
                    Bridget Cherry & Nikolaus Pevsner, Penguin, 1998, pp 267-8.

8.   The Smith & Brewer papers are held at the Alexander Architectural Archive at the University of Texas, Austin, Texas. The drawings for BCH were discovered during research in 2004 by Karen Butti, who surmises plausibly that the drawings (which were made by one of Smith & Brewer's assistants) were probably done for BCH at the instance of Mrs Humphry Ward (Mrs Creighton's old friend), for whom the partnership did a lot of work, not least including the University Hall Settlement, which she funded. Karen Butti further speculates, "I wonder if Smith & Brewer just drew up a rough scheme as a favour to the Settlement, with the builder left to work out all the details. It was obviously done on a tight budget, or something more permanent than boarding would probably have been used to infill the street windows." She also points out that both Smith and Brewer had been Settlement residents in their youth, so were presumably sympathetic.
(Letter to BCH Director Karen Osborn, 1 September 2004, in BCH 'Building Plans' Folder). The link to the University of Texas Archive is:
www.lib.utexas.edu/taro/utaaa/00046/aaa-00046.html

9.   LH, DD/531, Box 1 [BCH1/25A].

10.   LH, DD/531, Box 1 [BCH2/1/2, meeting of 22 March, 1923].

11.   *The Story of Bishop Creighton House*, C. M. L. Wickham & F. E. Hansford,
                    Fulham History Society, 1965, p 4.

12.   LH, DD/531, Box 1 [BCH1/4 p 6].

13.   LH, DD/531, Box 1 [BCH1/3 p 4].

14.   *Toynbee Hall - The First Hundred Years*, Asa Briggs & Anne Macartney,
                    Routledge & Kegan Paul, 1984, p 63.

15.   LH, DD/531, Box 1 [BCH1/5 pp 5-6].

16.   LH, DD/531, Box 1 [BCH1/6 pp 7-8].

17.   LH, DD/531, Box 1 [BCH1/5 p 7].

CHAPTER SIX - "KEEP THE HOME FIRES BURNING"

1.   LH, DD/531, Box 1 [BCH1/8 p 3].

2.   LH, DD/531, Box 1 [BCH1/7 p 8].

NOTES pp 43-57
3.   LH, DD/531, Box 1 [BCH1/8 p 7].
4.   LH, DD/531, Box 1 [BCH1/11 p 2].
5.   LH, DD/531, Box 1 [BCH2/1/1].
CHAPTER SEVEN - "THE DESIGN OF THE INSTITUTION SHALL BE…"
1.   Letter to Warden Daisy Wilson, 15 November 1956, found in
    BCH Archive folder: 'History, Constitution - Various Papers.'
2.   LH, DD/531, Box 1 [BCH2/1/2].
3.   BCH Archive folder: 'History, Constitution - Various Papers.'
4.   Ibid.
5.   LH, DD/531, Box 1 [BCH1/31 p 8].
6.   BCH Archive folder: 'History, Constitution - Various Papers.'
    Miss Harry to Messrs Pollard, Cooper & Thorowgood, 18 March 1943.
7.   Ibid, R. W. S. Pollard to Miss Harry, 26 March 1943.
    Mr Pollard actually referred to 'Clause 30' in his letter, but that was
    evidently a typing error.
8.   LH, DD/531, Box 1 [BCH1/44 p 16].
9.   BCH Council Minutes, 7 February 1951 to 7 November 1962,
                    meeting of 5 November 1952.
10.   Ibid, meeting of 5 June 1957.
CHAPTER EIGHT - VIGILANCE
1.   LH, DD/531, Box 1 [BCH1/16 p 4].
2.   LH, DD/531, Box 1 [BCH2/1/1, meeting of 15 January 1917].
3.   LH, DD/531, Box 1 [BCH1/16 p 4].
4.   LH, DD/531, Box 1 [BCH1/17 p 3].
5.   Ibid, p 10.
6.   LH, DD/531, Box 1 [BCH1/18 p 4].
7.   LH, DD/531, Box 3 [BCH3/5/4].
8.   BCH Council Minutes, 7 May 1936 to 10December 1941,
                    meeting of 10 December 1941.
9.   LH, DD/531, Box 1 [BCH2/1/3 meeting of 14 July 1926].
10.   Ibid, meeting of 6 October 1926.
11.   Ibid, meeting of 27 October 1926.
12.   LH, DD/531, Box 1 [BCH1/19 p 3].
13.   LH, DD/531, Box 3 [BCH3/3/9].
14.   LH, DD/531, Box 1 [BCH1/16 p 14].
15.   LH, DD/531, Box 1 [BCH1/22 pp 11-12].
16.   LH, DD/531, Box 1 [BCH1/21 pp 13-14].
17.   LH, DD/531, Box 1 [BCH1/20 p 5].
18.   LH, DD/531, Box 1 [BCH1/73 p 7].
19.   LH, DD/531, Box 1 [BCH1/24 p 3].
    This boy was anticipating another CCHF holiday beneficiary in 1954,
    who returned from the trip and informed his parents, "There are apples
    off of trees, not barrers." (LH, DD/531, Box 1 [BCH1/47 p 12]).
20.   LH, DD/531, Box 1 [BCH1/20 p 12].

NOTES pp 58-67
CHAPTER NINE - THE PREMISES
1. LH, DD/531, Box 1 [BCH1/61 p 4]. Miss Wickham writing, in the Annual Report for 1968-69, a tribute to her sister Christian, who died 1 December 1968, aged 90.
2. LH, DD/531, Box 1 [BCH1/18 p 2].
3. Miss Russell and her cousin, Miss Anley, joined BCH in 1915 and worked twenty years, retiring with Miss Wickham in 1935. Apart from her, they were the longest-serving workers in BCH history, and Miss Wickham had no doubt they were most important contributors to the BCH community. She wrote of them, "Having full-time jobs, they could only offer evenings and weekends, but before long they had decided to give all their time to the Settlement and to make it their home. Miss Anley sacrificed a highly-paid post and, instead, received a small salary as Club Leader. Up to then residents had been entirely voluntary, except the Warden who had always had free board and lodging. Later on Miss Russell was also given free board as Bursar, and later still a small salary for undertaking the management of the Clinic."
4. LH, DD/531, Box 1 [BCH1/20 p 3].
5. LH, DD/531, Box 1 [BCH2/1/3 meeting of 13 December 1928].
6. LH, DD/531, Box 3 [BCH3/3/12]
7. LH, DD/531, Box 3 [BCH4/5/3/1]
8. LH, DD/531, Box 1 [BCH1/27 p 5].
9. LH, DD/531, Box 1 [BCH1/29 pp 26-7].
10. LH, DD/531, Box 1 [BCH1/30 p 18].
11. LH, DD/531, Box 2 [BCH2/6].
12. Ibid.
13. Ibid.
14. Ibid.
15. LH, DD/531, Box 1 [BCH1/30 p 13].
16. BCH Council Minutes 7 May 1936 to 10 December 1941, meeting of 6 October 1938.
17. LH, DD/531, Box 1 [BCH1/31 p 17].
18. BCH 'Memories' Folder, letter of 18 November 1990.
19. Interview, 13 February 2008.
20. BCH 'Memories' Folder, talk at the Women's Club AGM, 3 April 2000.
21. LH, DD/531, Box 1 [BCH1/30 p 14].
22. LH, DD/531, Box 1 [BCH1/31 p 18].
23. LH, DD/531, Box 1 [BCH1/26 p 4].
24. LH, DD/531, Box 1 [BCH1/30 p 20].
25. LH, DD/531, Box 1 [BCH1/22 loose insert].
26. LH, DD/531, Box 1 [BCH1/23 pp 3-4].
27. LH, DD/531, Box 1 [BCH1/45 p 8].
28. Sky Fever, Sir Geoffrey de Havilland, Hamish Hamilton, 1961, pp 52 & 56. There is also in the book a photograph of Sir Geoffrey's wife sewing fabric for the fuselage in the Fulham workshop, against a whitewashed brick wall.
CHAPTER TEN - "NOT IN ALL RESPECTS REASONABLY FIT..."
1. This quotation, from an anonymous Fulham resident, and the Chapter Title are both extracted from the REPORT OF HOUSING CONDITIONS IN THE METROPOLITAN BOROUGH OF FULHAM by Irene T. Barclay and Evelyn E. Perry, published by BCH and the Fulham Christian Social Council, October 1927. LBHF Archives, F331.83. Hereafter cited as REPORT.

NOTES pp 67-81

2.   LH, DD/531, Box 1 [BCH1/19 p 6].
3.   LH, F333.324, Fulham Housing Association, 40th Annual Report.
4.   REPORT, op cit, p 8.
5.   Ibid, pp 9-10. The report does not give the house number, to guard the residents' privacy; but it gives pause for thought to know, eighty years on, that these same houses on this short street are, on average, fetching nearly £600,000.
6.   Ibid, pp 16-17.
7.   Ibid, p 23.
8.   Miss Wickham's obituary of Miss Lupton, cited at n3 above.
9.   LH, DD/193.
10.   Ibid.
11.   LH, DD/531, Box 1 [BCH2/1/3 meeting of 17 April 1929].
12.   LH, DD/531, Box 1 [BCH1/21 p 3].
13.   LH, DD/531, Box 1 [BCH1/22 p 3].
14.   LH, DD/531, Box 1 [BCH1/24 p 6].
15.   *The History of Fulham*, edited by P. D. Whitting,
          published by the Fulham History Society, 1970, pp 95-6.
16.   LH, DD/531, Box 1 [BCH1/30 p 16].
17.   BCH Council Minutes 2 January 1963 to 2 July 1969,
          meeting of 8 September 1965.

CHAPTER ELEVEN - EMERGENCY

1.   LH, DD/531, Box 3 [BCH5/5/17].
2.   BCH Council Minutes 7 May 1936 to 10 December 1941,
          meeting of 6 October 1938.
3.   Ibid, meeting of 30 January 1940.
4.   Ibid, meeting of 27 September 1939.
5.   LH, DD/531, Box 1 [BCH1/33 p 1].
6.   BCH Council Minutes 7 May 1936 to 10 December 1941,
          meeting of 19 September 1940.
7.   BCH 'Memories' Folder, Letter from Cyril Hollingbery, 12 July 1990.
8.   BCH Council Minutes 7 May 1936 to 10 December 1941,
          meeting of 15 October 1940.
9.   LH, DD/531, Box 3 [BCH5/5/17].
10.   BCH 'Memories' Folder, Letter from Helen Macdonald, nd.
11.   *Fulham Chronicle*, 31 July 1942. Pasted in BCH Council Minutes.
12.   LH, DD/531, Box 1 [BCH1/34 p 10].
13.   Ibid, p 11.
14.   LH, DD/531, Box 1 [BCH1/36 p 5].
15.   Ibid, same page.
16.   Ibid, same page.
17.   Ibid, p 6.
18.   BCH Council Minutes 14 January 1942 to 6 December 1944,
          Club Report July 1944 stapled in.
19.   LH, DD/531, Box 1 [BCH1/37 p 5].
20.   Ibid, p 8.

NOTES to pp 83-97

CHAPTER TWELVE - THE GREEN TREE
1. LH, DD/531, Box 3 [BCH5/4/11 p 18]. 'Report on the Green Tree House', hereafter 'GT Report.' Anyone who goes to the original roughly-typed document will notice that I have taken, for the sake of clarity, minor liberties with Miss Kruse's English.
2. Ibid, p 1.
3. Ibid, pp 1-2.
4. LH, DD/531, Box 3 [BCH5/3/1 is the correspondence about Fr Kruse].
5. GT Report, pp 10-11.
6. Ibid, pp 12-13.
7. Ibid, pp 14-15.
8. Ibid, pp 15-16.
9. Ibid, pp 18-19.
10. Ibid, pp 24-26.
11. LH, DD/531, Box 2 [BCH2/8, meeting of 27 February 1947].
12. GT Report, p 27.
13. BCH Council Minutes 7 February 1945 to 6 December 1950, meeting of 11 June 1947.
14. Ibid, meeting of 2 July 1947.
15. Ibid, meeting of 3 September 1947.
16. Ibid, meeting of 1 October 1947.

CHAPTER THIRTEEN - SOCIAL REVOLUTION
1. LH, DD/531, Box 1 [BCH1/42 p 12].
2. LH, DD/531, Box 1 [BCH1/38 p 2].
3. BCH Council & Committee Minutes 7 February 1945 to 6 December 1950, Report presented to Council 1 October 1947.
4. LH, DD/531, Box 1 [BCH1/43 pp 10-11].
5. LH, DD/531, Box 1 [BCH1/42 p 9].
6. LH, DD/531, Box 1 [BCH1/45 pp 11-12].
7. LH, DD/531, Box 1 [BCH1/45 pp 3-4].
8. Interview, 13 February 2008.
9. LH, DD/531, Box 1 [BCH1/31 p 11].
    Worth mentioning in passing that T. S. Eliot, no less, gave a poetry reading in October 1934 at the home of a BCH Council member to raise funds for the Skilled Employment & Apprenticeship Committee. No doubt it was 'just a piece of rhythmical grumbling.'
10. BCH Council Minutes 7 February 1951 to 7 November 1962, meeting of 5 February 1958.
11. BCH Council Minutes 2 January 1963 to 2 July 1969, meeting of 4 June 1969.
12. BCH Council Minutes 10 September 1969 to 5 July 1972, meeting of 10 September 1969.

CHAPTER FOURTEEN - YOUTH
1. BCH Council Minutes 7 February 1951 to 7 November 1962, meeting of 16 September 1959.
2. Ibid, meeting of 6 March 1957.

3.   It is worth recalling of Fenner Brockway that, during the Conservatives'
      'thirteen years of misrule,' 1951-1964, he unsuccessfully introduced a bill every year
      for nine years to make racial discrimination illegal, which was eventually passed in
      1965 early in Harold Wilson's premiership.
3.   BCH Council Minutes 7 February 1951 to 7 November 1962,
                          Warden's report to Council, 5 February 1958.
4.   Ibid, meeting of 17 February 1960.
5.   Ibid, meeting of 16 November 1960.
6.   Ibid, meeting of 7 November 1962.
7.   BCH Council Minutes 2 January 1963 to 2 July 1969,
                          meeting of 2 October 1963.
8.   Ibid, meeting of 2 October 1963.
9.   Ibid, meeting of 6 November 1963.
10.   Ibid, meeting of 5 February 1964.
11.   Ibid, meeting of 3 February 1965.
12.   Ibid, meeting of 6 April 1966.
13.   Ibid, meeting of 14 September 1966.
14.   Ibid, meeting of 7 December 1966.
15.   Ibid, meeting of 4 October 1967.
16.   Ibid, meeting of 5 June 1968.
17.   Ibid, meeting of 5 February 1969.
18.   Ibid, meeting of 5 March 1969.
19.   Ibid, meeting of 7 May 1969.
20.   BCH Council Minutes 10 September 1969 to 5 July 1972,
                          meeting of 1 October 1969.
21.   Ibid, meeting of 3 December 1969.
22.   Ibid, meeting of 4 February 1970.
23.   Ibid, meeting of 4 March 1970.
24.   Ibid, meeting of 15 September 1971.
25.   Ibid, meeting of 5 July 1972.
26.   BCH Youth Project, Report on the First Two Years, January 1978, pp 5-6.
27.   Ibid, p 16.
28.   Ibid, p 17.
29.   BCH Council & Committee Minutes 6 September 1972 to 3 March 1982,
      Executive Committee meeting, 3 July 1980.
30.   BCH Council & Committee Minutes 31 March 1982 to 5 December 1984,
                          Director's Report to Executive Committee, 5 September 1984.
31.   Ibid, Director's Report to Council, 7 November 1984.
32.   BCH Council and Committee Minutes 9 January 1985 to 4 December 1991,
                          Report to Council, 1 February 1989.
33.   Ibid, Discussion Paper presented to Council, 6 June 1990.
34.   LH, DD/531, Box 1 [BCH1/82 p 8].

CHAPTER FIFTEEN - WOMEN

1.   *Life & Letters of Mandell Creighton*, Louise Creighton,
                          2 Volumes, Longmans Green, 1904, 1:99.
2.   LH, DD/531, Box 2 BCH2/5.
3.   LH, DD/531, Box 1 [BCH1/31 p 21].
4.   LH, DD/531, Box 1 [BCH1/49 pp 5-6].
5.   LH, DD/531, Box 1 [BCH1/60 p 8].
6.   LH, DD/531, Box 1 [BCH1/44 p 7].

NOTES pp 106-116
7.   LH, DD/531, Box 1, [BCH1/52 p 7].
8.   LH, DD/531, Box 1 [BCH1/45 pp 6-7].
9.   LH, DD/531, Box 1 [BCH1/47 pp 7-8].
10.   LH, DD/531, Box 1 [BCH1/61 p 8].
11.   LH, DD/531, Box 1 [BCH1/86 p 8].
12.   LH, DD/531, Box 1 [BCH1/35 p 4].
13.   LH, DD/531, Box 1 [BCH1/36 p 3].
14.   LH, DD/531, Box 1 [BCH1/54 p 7].
15.   LH, DD/531, Box 1 [BCH1/60 p 7].
CHAPTER SIXTEEN - WHAT ARE SETTLEMENTS FOR?
1.   LH, DD/531, Box 1 [BCH1/29 p 14].
2.   *The Spectator*, 21 December 1934.
3.   LH, DD/531, Box 1 [BCH1/29 p 14].
4.   *The Social Worker*, Clement Attlee, G. Bell & Sons, 1920, p 216.
5.   BCH Council & Committee Minutes 14 May 1929 to 17 July 1935,
          meeting of 18 March 1932.
6.   BCH Council & Committee Minutes 7 May 1936 to 10 December 1941,
          meeting of 10 December 1941.
7.   BCH Council & Committee Minutes 7 February 1945 to 6 December 1950,
          meeting of 12 November 1945.
8.   The Federation of Residential Settlements was founded in 1920 with 40
      members. Renamed BARS in the 1930s, it was again renamed as BASSAC
      (British Association of Settlements & Social Action Centres) in 1978,
      and presently has over 100 members. From 1961 to 1970 the BARS
      secretariat was headquartered at BCH.
9.   BCH Council & Committee Minutes 7 May 1936 to 10 December 1941,
          BARS Memorandum bound in September 1941.
10.   BCH Council & Committee Minutes 7 May 1936 to 10 December 1941,
          resumé of Conference presented to Council, 5 November 1941.
11.   LH, DD/531, Box 1 [BCH1/38 pp 3-4].
12.   LH, DD/531, Box 1 [BCH1/46 pp 5 & 17-18].
13.   BCH Council Minutes 7 February 1951 to 7 November 1962,
          meeting of 2 May 1962.
14.   BCH Council Minutes 2 January 1963 to 2 July 1969,
          meeting of 1 February 1967.
15.   Ibid, meeting of 5 April 1967.
16.   LH, DD/531, Box 1 [BCH1/72 p 3].
17.   LH, DD/531, Box 1 [BCH1/81 p 2].
18.   BCH Council & Committee Minutes 8 January 1992 to 5 March 1997,
          Executive Committee meeting of 6 March 1996.
19.   LH, DD/531, Box 1 [BCH1/89 p 2].
20.   LH, DD/531, Box 1 [BCH1/76 p 3].
CHAPTER SEVENTEEN - KEEPING IT UP
1.   Speaking at a service in All Saints Church, Fulham, to celebrate BCH's
      40th birthday, 22 May 1948.
2.   *The Story of Bishop Creighton House*, Wickham, C. M. L. & Hansford, F. E.
          Fulham History Society Publication No 5, 1965, p 4.
3.   *The Social Worker*, Clement Attlee, G. Bell & Sons, 1920, p 135.
4.   LH, DD/531, Box 1 [BCH1/59 p 7].

NOTES pp 116-124

5.   LH, DD/531, Box 1 [BCH1/63 p 13].
6.   LH, DD/531, Box 1 [BCH1/65 p 13].
7.   LH, DD/531, Box 1 [BCH1/60 pp 20-1].
8.   LH, DD/531, Box 1 [BCH1/63 p 10].
9.   LH, DD/531, Box 1 [BCH1/80 p 18].
10.   LH, DD/531, Box 1 [BCH1/81 p 10].
11.   LH, DD/531, Box 1 [BCH1/82 p 6].
12.   LH, DD/531, Box 1 [BCH1/85 pp 9-10].
13.   LH, DD/531, Box 1 [BCH1/87 p 5].
14.   BCH Board of Trustees Minutes 2 April 1997 to 4 July 2001,
                                meeting of 6 October 1999.
15.   BCH Board of Trustees Minutes 5 September 2001 to 2 March 2005,
                                meeting of 3 September 2003.
16.   BCH 96th Annual Report, 2004.
17.   BCH 98th Annual Report, 2006.
18.   LH, DD/531, Box 1 [BCH1/74 p 3].
19.   LH, DD/531, Box 1 [BCH1/76 p 12].
20.   LH, DD/531, Box 1 [BCH1/81 p 12].
21.   LH, DD/531, Box 1 [BCH1/82 p 7].
22.   LH, DD/531, Box 1 [BCH1/85 p 10].
23.   LH, DD/531, Box 1 [BCH1/85 p 8].
24.   BCH 94th Annual Report, 2001-2002.
25.   Clement Attlee speech   31 March 1947. Quoted in *Toynbee Hall*, Asa Briggs and
        Anne Macartney, Routledge & Kegan Paul, 1984, pp 135-6.

***

BIBLIOGRAPHY

Attlee, Clement *The Social Worker*   G. Bell & Sons, 1920

Barnett, Samuel & Henrietta *Practicable Socialism*   2nd Ed., Rev., Longmans, 1894

Barnett, Henrietta *Canon Barnett - His Life, Work, and Friends*   John Murray, 1918

Beveridge, William *Voluntary Action*   Allen & Unwin, 1948

Beveridge, William *Power & Influence*   Hodder & Stoughton, 1953

Booth, Charles *Life and Labour of the People in London* 3rd Series
Volume 3: *The City of London and the West End* Macmillan, 1902

Bosanquet, Helen *Social Work in London*   John Murray, 1914

Briggs, Asa and Macartney, Anne *Toynbee Hall*   Routledge & Kegan Paul, 1984

Chadwick, Owen *The Victorian Church*   2 Vols, A&C Black, 1966 & 1970

Covert, James *A Victorian Marriage - Mandell & Louise Creighton*
     Hambledon and London, 2000

Creighton, Louise *Memoir of a Victorian Woman: Reflections of Louise Creighton*
     Edited by James Covert, Indiana University Press, 1994

Creighton, Louise *Women's Settlements* (Article)
     The Nineteenth Century, Vol 63, April 1908

Creighton, Louise *Life & Letters of Mandell Creighton*   2 Vols, Longmans, 1904

Creighton, Mandell *University and Other Sermons* Longmans, 1903

Fallows, W. G. *Mandell Creighton and the English Church*   OUP, 1964

Free, Rev[d]. Richard *Settlements or Unsettlements?* (article)
     The Nineteenth Century, Vol 63, March 1908

Fulham History Society *A History of Fulham*   FHS, 1970

Gosse, Edmund *Portraits & Sketches*   Heinemann, 1912

Green, John Richard *Stray Studies*   Macmillan, 1903

Heeney, Brian *The Women's Movement in the CoE 1850-1930* Oxford, 1988

Humphreys, Robert *Poor Relief and Charity 1869-1945* Palgrave, 2001

Kitson Clark, George *Churchmen and the Condition of England 1832-1885*
     Methuen, 1973

Leighton, Sir Baldwyn (Ed) *Letters & Other Writings of the late Edward Denison*
     Richard Bentley, 1872

Lewis, Jane *Women and Social Action in Victorian and Edwardian England*
     Edward Elgar, Aldershot, 1991

Meacham, Standish *Toynbee Hall and Social Reform 1880-1914* Yale, 1987

Mearns, Andrew *The Bitter Cry of Outcast London*
     A. S. Wohl (Ed), rp Leicester University Press, 1970

Nevinson, Henry *Changes and Chances* Nisbet, 1923

Okey, T. *A Basketful of Memories* Dent, 1930

Rooff, Madeline *A Hundred Years of Family Welfare* Michael Joseph, 1972

Stedman Jones, Gareth *Outcast London*   Clarendon, Oxford, 1971

Strachey, Lytton *Portraits in Miniature* Chatto & Windus, 1931

Webb, Beatrice *My Apprenticeship*   Longmans Green, 1926

Webb, Beatrice *Our Partnership*   Longmans Green, 1948

Whelan, Robert *Helping the Poor*   Civitas, 2001

Wickham, C. M. L. & Hansford, F. E. *The Story of Bishop Creighton House*
     Fulham History Society Publication No 5, 1965

Young, A. F. and Ashton, E. T. *British Social Work in the Nineteenth Century*
     Routledge & Kegan Paul, 1956

144